There Are
No Simple Answers

A TRIBUTE
TO
ARCHBISHOP PETER LEO GERETY, D.D.

Cassian J. Yuhaus, C.P. H.E.D.
Editor

Preface by
Joseph Cardinal Bernardin, D.D.

PAULIST PRESS
New York and Mahwah, N.J.

Cover design by Moe Berman.

Copyright © 1996 by Cassian J. Yuhaus, C.P. H.E.D.

All rights reserved. No part of this book may be reproduced or transmitted in any form or by any means, electronic or mechanical, including photocopying, recording or by any information storage and retrieval system without permission in writing from the Publisher.

Library of Congress Cataloging-in-Publication Data

There are no simple answers : a tribute to archbishop Peter Leo Gerety, D.D. /
    Cassian J. Yuhaus, C.P. H.E.D., editor.
        p.   cm.
    ISBN 0-8091-3658-9
    1. Gerety, Peter Leo. 2. Catholic Church—United States—Bishops—Biography. 3.
United States—Church history. I. Yuhaus, Cassian J.
BX4705.G4244T44 1995
282′.092—dc20   95-26712
[B]   CIP

Published by Paulist Press
997 Macarthur Boulevard
Mahwah, NJ 07430

Printed and bound in the
United States of America

Contents

Preface

His Eminence, Joseph Cardinal Bernardin, D.D.
Archbishop of Chicago

I was very happy to hear that several friends of Archbishop Gerety had spontaneously turned to one another one evening and said quite simply, "Let's put together a little tribute to a wonderful man and a great priest." I was delighted when they asked me to write a preface for their book. I am honored to do so.

By every measure the life and work of Peter Leo Gerety is an extraordinary achievement. His priestly life falls into two almost equal periods: twenty-three years as pastor of a challenging inner-city parish in New Haven and twenty years as Bishop and Archbishop. But there were not two different tasks or two distinct careers. They were all one: being a priest, a true priest, a committed priest from beginning to end.

This thoughtful book is filled with wonderful reflections on the Archbishop's life and ministry. They are refreshing and encouraging. My own brief reflection will touch upon several of these and draw as well upon my personal friendship with Archbishop Gerety.

I like very much what Professor Liddy wrote in his contribution, "The Passionateness of Being." He says that one of the major characteristics of being is that "it is a call heard within our own very spirit." Furthermore, he says that this is a call "to move beyond what seems to be to what is...beyond what merely 'feels good' to what is good." He concludes with this challenging truth: "Once we arrive at what is true and good...the die is cast; our very being calls us to move in that direction."

As a young man, Peter Gerety arrived at what is true and good: the priesthood of Jesus Christ. The die was cast, and with all his being he never ceased moving with alacrity and conviction in that direction.

1

This was also true when he moved into the inner-city and took up the cause of the poor and dispossessed Black and Hispanic minorities. He was one of the first priests to do so in this country. While already fluent in French, he quickly learned Spanish in order to be one with his people and strong in their defense. This was true when, in the midst of conflicting opinions, he carried the fight for funding for the National Office for Black Catholics to the floor of the National Conference of Catholic Bishops. There he argued successfully with courage and conviction on the legitimacy of the NOBC request. This was also true when he moved to the Archdiocese of Newark and confronted the existing $40 million dollar debt, seeking justice, distinguishing between legitimate claims and dubious ones, between those that were primary and those that were tertiary, and finally, with great perspicacity and daring, resolving the entire debt.

This was also true in 1975 when he listened as a *bonus pastor*, a good shepherd, to the cries and the pain of separated, divorced, and remarried Catholics. For the first time in our country, he courageously established an official agency of the Archdiocese to serve these people with special needs, naming it Ministry to Divorced Catholics.

There are many other distinctive and courageous acts, but I will name only one more and then offer some reflections on the overall tone and character of his career as a priest and leader of God's people. When Archbishop Gerety moved to Newark he found one of the finest interdiocesan seminaries at Darlington, NJ, located in a beautiful rural setting with a number of attractive and well-constructed buildings. After a thorough study and professional analysis of the situation, however, he moved the seminary into the city, connecting it with a vibrant university, Seton Hall. There he revamped its entire administrative and formation program.

The overall tone and character of his episcopal career is best reflected in a concern that became his major preoccupation, we might even say his obsession: the Second Vatican Council. This preoccupation found a very direct expression in a vast project that his uncanny sense for "the-right-thing-at-the-right-time" caused him to embrace, support, develop, and foster until the day of his retirement. That project is RENEW.

Peter Gerety was ordained Coadjutor Bishop of Portland, Maine, June 1, 1966, less than one year after the close of the Second Vatican Council. He made it his primary task to implement this historic transformational event in the history of Catholicism. He studied every page of the sixteen major documents of the Council in their original and official language, Latin. He was further helped by the abundant periodical and research literature from France since he was fluent in French and had studied at St. Sulpice in Paris.

In his moving contribution to this *Festschrift*, Bishop Joseph Francis, D.D., S.V.D., speaks so vividly of his commitment to the teaching and spirit of the Council: "As I observed this giant of a man taking on the challenges of his time, it suddenly dawned on me that for so many years I had looked upon Bishops as aloof and distant individuals who…could be approached by only a few…Archbishop Gerety changed all that for me…as (his) auxiliary I entered into a new and intense world of ministry. All of the dreams I had of how Vatican II should and would be implemented began to become a reality." And then Bishop Francis concludes this reflection with the forthright declaration: "At last I found a Bishops' Bishop and a priests' Bishop and a people's Bishop whose only ambition was to make the Church of Newark come alive in the last quarter of the twentieth century."

Archbishop Gerety made Vatican II a reality by restructuring archdiocesan pastoral and administrative services, developing an administrative style based upon subsidiarity and collaborative ministry, encouraging creativity, beginning the ministry to priest program, welcoming and supporting women in ministry, calling forth youth to active ministry, and generously releasing priests and encouraging laity to serve the larger Church in the U.S. and throughout the world. His was indeed a new vision of the Church, the New Pentecost foreseen by John XXIII and heralded by the Second Vatican Council.

Even a casual observer stands in awe at what one small group of priests and people, supported and encouraged by a visionary—indeed, a prophetic—Archbishop, could achieve through RENEW. Monsignor Thomas A. Kleissler has written an excellent summary of the contributions of this quiet movement to the Church. His colleague, Monsignor Thomas Ivory, gives us clear insight into its theology and sound ecclesiology. We are indebted to both authors for this refreshing summation of a truly great movement in our time.

RENEW has been embraced and implemented in 126 dioceses of the United States and in 98 dioceses in fourteen other countries around the world from the South Pacific through Europe to Africa and Central America.

Again, in RENEW we see a characteristic interest of Archbishop Gerety: the formation and training of small Christian groups to become communities of faith-in-action. As Monsignor Kleissler states, "Among the values Archbishop Gerety saw in small communities was their effectiveness as an instrument for the formation of our society and assistance to the poor and needy. He also saw small communities as an extremely effective means to be about the work of evangelization. It is precisely these convictions in his pastoral legacy that we so badly need to keep before us today."

I am very grateful for this work. It brings to mind in such a refreshing way the enormity of the challenge facing all of us who exercise a leadership role in a time of major transformation for Church and society. In his always quiet and unobtrusive way, never commanding, never demanding, but always encouraging, recommending, and challenging, Archbishop Gerety gives us a model of leadership for post-conciliar times, true to Christ, true to his Church, true to his priesthood.

He would wait patiently in hope and prayer that we too would hear the call "within our own very spirit, and...move beyond appearances... beyond what seems to be to what is" until we too have grasped the true and the good. Then the die is cast, and we move unflinchingly toward its attainment.

Foreword

Most Rev. Theodore E. McCarrick, Ph.D., D.D.
Archbishop of Newark, N.J.

In today's American society, what makes an outstanding Bishop? Perhaps more than anything else, it is the courage to pursue a vision of the Church that is at one and the same time faithful to the teaching of the Gospel and responsive to the needs of our times. By any measure which takes those criteria into account, Peter Leo Gerety has been an outstanding shepherd.

Those of us who have had the privilege of being close to him over the years have witnessed the depth of his own personal faith and love of the Church, as we have also seen his deep convictions about the Church's need to respond to the concerns and even the sometimes tragic realities of urban America.

When Archbishop Gerety came to Newark in 1974, he found a community still scarred from the terrible social upheavals of the late 1960's. He found a Church trying its best to cope with these problems and to come to grips with the new demographic and economic reality of a changed northeastern New Jersey. The Archbishop brought his strength and his clear vision to this task. He knew that the Church needed to continue and accelerate its openness to the new racial and ethnic realities it faced, and that this would take resources of both personnel and finance.

By affirming and fostering the process of RENEW, he prepared a whole new generation of Catholic lay leaders—and had the vision to see that this process could serve in other dioceses throughout the country and indeed throughout the world—and by attacking the serious financial crisis of the Archdiocese, he strove to get a handle on the Church's ability to continue to support its pastoral and charitable services.

In the early years of his time as our Archbishop, Archbishop Gerety had to be a skilled and valiant juggler, keeping the ship afloat financially while responding to the needs of his people, especially in the new environment of the post Vatican II Church and the post civil disturbances community in which he worked. As I look back on those days of challenge from the vantage point of a decade since his retirement, I am truly filled with wonder at his strength and his ability. He found great partners in the lay community where he encouraged outstanding leaders to work at his side. In spite of obstacles, he moved steadily forward and didn't miss a beat.

In his retirement, with the tangible accomplishments of his years as Archbishop of Newark behind him, the local Church has grown to know him in a new and even richer way. Our Catholic people and our neighbors have now seen this strong and dynamic leader as a warm and faithful priest, a generous friend and a constant and perspective student of the Church and society.

I welcome this initiative to prepare a Festschrift in his honor. As a scholar and a doer, and as an outstanding Bishop, Peter Leo Gerety deserves no less than such a tribute from those of us who continue to be grateful for what the Lord has accomplished through his labors.

1

An Archbishop for Our Time

Franklyn M. Casale

In 1974 the Archdiocese of Newark was in the unusual state of trying to interpret and implement the results of an Ecumenical Council. The times were more challenging than anyone had ever anticipated. On June 19, 1974, Bishop Peter L. Gerety came to us from Maine.

As with most public personalities, a bit of a reputation preceded him. He was known to be dedicated to the progressive renewal of the Church. We knew he was pastoral because of his 23 years of pastoring the people of St. Martin De Porres Church in the inner-city of New Haven, Connecticut, and his involvement in social justice issues nationally. People considered him somewhat erudite since he studied at St. Sulpice in Paris, speaking and reading French fluently. Father Gerety had also mastered Spanish in order to minister more intimately to the people in New Haven.

Very quickly the people of the Newark Archdiocese learned more about their Archbishop. We came to know him as a man of vision, interpreting the intent of the Vatican Council as one of pastoral improvement. His mission was the building up of the body of Christ with single-minded purpose through dedicated service.

The administrative problems in the Archdiocese of Newark needed to be dealt with quickly and aggressively so that pastoral programs could be supported. The Archbishop attacked the enormous deficit, addressed the administrative structure, reorganized the University (Seton Hall) and created an effective system of pastoral governance with bishops, priests, and laity sharing responsibility. The administration soon came to be seen as one of expansion, not in the traditional sense of brick and mortar, but rather in terms of programs, and people were formed, served, educated, reconciled, and renewed.

The first twelve years saw many rapid changes, and characteristically Archbishop Gerety was the one leading the way, often leaving the rest of us who work with him rather breathless! We sensed, however, that he enjoyed the challenge and we, on our part, enjoyed being a part of the team.

The Archbishop's unique style for managing was one of delegation born of confidence in the people who worked with him. He was direct and determined. We always knew where we stood with him, a rare gift indeed! And, oh those questions with which he challenged us! He could pull a question out of thin air. Many times after a session with him, when some of us had felt a certain casual smugness, we were reminded that our Archbishop was always setting a standard of excellence.

When the credit was finally given, whether for clearing up the debt, fathering RENEW, writing pastorals on new and challenging subjects, he had a knack of stepping aside so that the accolades would be diffused among the staff. St. Paul characterized this approach to Church in the letter to the Corinthians: "The body is one and has many members, but all the members, many though they are, are one body: and so it is with Christ" (1 Cor. 12:12).

Archbishop Gerety presided at various functions or at the liturgy with quiet dignity and self-respect, leading us to clearly understand that there was a link with deep faith. Some of us would stumble upon him with a prayer book or rosary beads in the house, or in a dark corner of the Cathedral Chapel, on his knees in prayer. We realized that he is not only a man of ability, but also a man of prayer.

Archbishop Gerety is a bishop, as the Council says, who "exercises his office of father and pastor standing in the midst of his people as one who serves" (Decree on the Bishop's Pastoral Office in the Church, para. 16), and quite frankly, we are all proud to have served under him.

His episcopal motto, IN OMNIBUS CHRISTUS (Christ in everything), frames his ministerial life.

> ...and you have to put on a new self which will progress towards true knowledge the more it is renewed in the image of its creator; and in that image there is no room for distinction between Greek and Jew, between barbarian and Sycthian, slave and free man. There is only one Christ: he is everything and he is in everything (Col. 3:9–11).

Today we publicly express our thanks, respect, and affection to you, dear Archbishop Gerety. May God continue to bless your time of retirement and grant you health and happiness. Thank you for all you have given to us personally and to the Church of Newark.

2

A Church for the New Millennium

Thomas A. Kleissler

Back in the early seventies a magazine came out of Chicago called *The Critic* I remember the cover of one of its issues having a big clock and at each number on the clock there was a picture of a bishop who was considered to be a hope for the future church. For whatever reason my focus seemed to turn to eleven o'clock which was Bishop Peter L. Gerety of Portland, Maine.

On April 2, 1974, as I came out of my office someone announced to me, "A new archbishop has been assigned to Newark. It is Bishop Gerety of Portland, Maine." I was amazed having known only two archbishops of Newark in my entire life, Archbishop Walsh and Archbishop Boland, both of whom were natives of Newark. The idea of someone coming from outside the diocese was totally new. Of course this announcement came at a time when we were all waiting to see who our new archbishop would be. What a joy it was to know that at least one source considered him one of the great hopes for the future of the church.

It didn't take long to see that Archbishop Gerety was a man of great leadership. He was decisive and unafraid to move ahead and bite the bullet when a tough call needed to be made. You might say that this was clearly a man who knew how to get things done.

It was evident from the very beginning that Archbishop Gerety's overriding agenda was the implementation of Vatican II. Everything about his background would make this understandable. Here was a man who spent most of his years working as a parish priest. His work was largely in inner-city New Haven, Connecticut with Black and Hispanic communities. Interest in the poor, in people from various races and ethnic backgrounds, and the problems of everyday life were very real for Archbishop Gerety. After all, it was the daily stuff of which his priestly life consisted.

It was no surprise, therefore, that some of his earliest moves as Archbishop of Newark included setting a high priority on the development and formation of lay people, the encouragement of collaborative ministry and the establishment of councils that would bring together in mutual dialogue laity, members of religious communities, deacons, priests, and bishops.

Early on he initiated the formation of parish councils, deanery councils and the Newark Archdiocesan Pastoral Council. He recognized that these councils would only be effective to the extent that time and energy were put into the formation of the people comprising these bodies. That vision and insight helped lead to the creation and development of the RENEW process.

Very essential to the RENEW process was the development of small faith-sharing groups, something that Archbishop Gerety heartily endorsed. Whereas in the late 70's many priests were somewhat hesitant about endorsing small faith-sharing groups, there was no hesitancy on the part of the Archbishop. His pastoral experience assured him that this was a vehicle that would not only assist the spiritual development of people but also better enable them to carry out their Christian responsibilities in the world. On a number of occasions he made a point of noting that the renewal of the church had always come about from small communities of people.

Among the values Archbishop Gerety saw in small communities was their effectiveness as an instrument for the formation of our society and assistance to the poor and needy. He also saw small communities as an extremely effective means to be about the work of evangelization. It is precisely these convictions in his pastoral legacy that we so badly need to keep before us today.

Small communities now have achieved a great degree of acceptance. However, the suggestion here is that they do not really deserve the title of "small Christian communities" unless they effectively include a strong mission thrust that is characterized by a deep caring and an effective involvement in responding to the needs of people and the injustices confronting our world today.

Fifty years ago, small communities of people coming together to share faith were not a common occurrence in parish life. They were very much a peripheral activity, the kind of thing that zealots and

Catholic Action people were involved in. As time transpired some even developed a fear of small communities because of what they perceived as excesses of social actions involvement in the base communities of Latin America. Today, however, the development of small Christian communities has become a central and major highlight in the agenda of dioceses in our country and around the world. In fact, it is not uncommon for bishops and church leaders to be working toward parishes being structured as communities made up of many small communities.

There are many reasons to believe that small communities represent a major hope for the future pastoral life of our church. All of this good promise, however, will turn to dust if an essential ingredient of community is ignored. To be healthy, small Christian communities must be about mission, with a strong commitment to outreach, the social teachings of the church and evangelization. Groups of people who come together and remain self-centered and satisfied in the joy and comfort they provide one another will eventually die of their own weight. The heart of the Christian message will be lost.

Regrettably much of what goes under the title of small Christian communities today is too similar to the discussion groups of decades past. While those discussion groups centered mostly on acquiring knowledge, today's groups tend to expand with a greater inclusion of sharing of life and faith experiences. This in itself is a very invigorating dynamic. While the nature of these groups tends to help participants bring faith out into everyday life they must at the same time combat a temptation to turn inward. Settling into a comfort zone would contradict our Christian call.

Even the popular idea that groups design their own content for their meetings and draw up their own questions from within has a built-in, glaring weakness. Anyone who has ever been deeply involved in the social mission of the church recognizes that many key issues and concerns highlighted in our church's teaching will not necessarily arise spontaneously. It is critically important that materials be designed that challenge people to thoroughly live the full gospel message. It would be naive to think that this will happen without a process carefully designed for growth and outreach.

The term, small Christian community, could well be applied only to communities that help people connect faith to every aspect of their lives. This would include family life, the larger community in which they live, the market place, and the larger world.

Community also implies that there has been a growth beyond group. Growth in becoming community will be especially evident where more trustful sharing, stronger support to one another, deeper spiritual growth, expanded learning of faith, and a wider sense of mission and outreach are developing.

Small Christian communities ought to be places where faith and life concerns not only intersect but where effective action is being carried out. To achieve this goal a wide range of materials for small communities' use is badly needed. Extended periods of time could be taken to develop concrete action in specific areas such as race relations, work, family life, parenting, sacramental preparation, women's rights and dignity, ecology, attitudes toward poverty, political responsibility, parish life, non-violence, the new cosmology, the homeless, world economy and the imbalance of the world's resources. This would help to bring into the forefront the social agenda of the church. Participants would be challenged to pray, study, gather information, and move into action in solidarity with one another and with other groups.

A return to the methodology of Observe, Judge, Act, so clearly set forth by St. Thomas Aquinas and so vigorously promoted by Cardinal Cardijn, would without doubt be a most effective way to bring about constructive action in many of these areas.

Cardijn's methodology has the strength through its "Observe" to help people deal concretely with attitudes and behaviors in the world around them rather than merely gather to discuss their own ideas and feelings. The "Judge" portion of this process enables people to look more closely at the attitudes and teachings of Christ as expressed in scripture along with church documents. It then invites participants to see more clearly what gaps may exist between the view of Christ and the realities dealt with in the Observe. The Judge aspect of the meeting then brings people to draw upon their collective wisdom in order to arrive at what precisely can be done to improve the given situation and to evolve a plan of how to go about it. This process, in a very natural way, leads to a commitment of a very definite action which may be done individually or by the community as a whole.

Everything said about how small Christian communities can be an effective means of implementing the Church's social teachings can also be applied to evangelization. For indeed, it is in evangelization that the transformation of culture spoken about by Paul VI can come about. Usual approaches of forming evangelizers through Sunday homilies or through individual training might mean resigning ourselves to a lengthy wait before seeing substantial progress. Even the development of parish evangelization committees or teams can too easily consign the work of evangelization to a particular group while letting the rest of the parish slide off the hook. The entire parish needs to be an evangelizing community.

The parish seen as a community made up of many small communities, with each community having an understanding of their evangelization responsibilities, would seem to be the surest way of realizing the collective baptismal calling. So often our backgrounds, upbringing, and society itself inhibit us from speaking openly about Christ and about our Catholic faith. The sharing of faith in small Christian communities not only deepens the faith commitment of each individual but also gives people the courage to more openly and confidently share with others in everyday life about their love for the Lord. How will we ever evangelize the world if we have not yet become free enough to speak about God and Jesus and their great love for us? For anyone who has been part of a faith-sharing community, it is hard to imagine a more effective means of achieving such outreach.

While sharing our faith is one thing, the hospitable welcoming and reception of people is still another. Even parishes with vital activity and rectories noted for their warmth can still appear distant and foreboding to someone looking on from a distance. Small informal community meetings, in the natural setting of living rooms, provide the most welcoming atmosphere one could hope to find. Hospitality is the first step of evangelization. Not only can small Christian communities become wonderful receiving places for inquirers but these small communities can also accompany candidates on every step of the catechumenal journey. Each person journeying toward full participation in the eucharistic community could be accompanied and supported at every step of the process not only by an individual sponsor but by a sponsoring community. What a glorious event the Easter Vigil would be as communities came forth to stand with and support each catechumen.

Post Mystagogia is another critical period. One American bishop, in speaking to his priests, said he feels good about how many people are coming in through the front door of our Church. Yet, he raised the question: "Is anyone watching the back door?" Well might he say this if the neophyte is cast into a lackluster parish experience that contrasts sharply with the very warm and communal catechumenal journey. The parish that is a community of small communities could incorporate neophytes into healthy small communities where they would grow in Christian life and ministry. Imagine how that neophyte would infuse the small community members with a fresh and lively faith.

The model of small Christian communities does offer an invigorating pastoral approach for our times. In our secular age there is no guarantee that faith will automatically be transferred and inherited. What is needed is an intentional faith the likes of which small Christian communities nurture and support.

Small Christian communities must go far beyond nurturing and support in order to assure a full Christian life of mission and evangelization. As Pope John Paul II says:

> A rapidly growing phenomenon in the young Churches…is that of "ecclesial basic communities" which are proving to be good centers for Christian formation and missionary outreach….Thus, these communities become a means of evangelization and of the initial proclamation of the Gospel and a source of new ministries. At the same time, by being imbued with Christ's love, they also show how divisions, tribalism and racism can be overcome. (Redemptoris Missio, #51, December 7, 1990)

Some of the basic principles that Archbishop Gerety promoted so vigorously in his tenure as an active shepherd are still as important and, perhaps, even more critically necessary for us to be a faithful people today.

3

Priestly Spirituality:
Then and Now

John Jay Hughes

The seminarian Peter Gerety, studying at St. Sulpice in Paris in the middle thirties, would surely have read the classic work of priestly spirituality, *The Soul of the Apostolate* by the Trappist Abbot Dom J.B. Chautard. Prior to Vatican II it was required reading for Catholic seminarians the world over. A revised edition of the French original, updated with references to the Vatican II documents, was published in France in 1979.[1] A reprint of the 1946 Gethsemane Abbey translation is still in print in the United States today.[2]

Vatican II incorporated the book's title into the fourth chapter of its Dogmatic Constitution on the Church. After stating that the laity share, through baptism and confirmation, in the Church's mission, the Council adds:

> Moreover, by the sacraments, especially by the Eucharist, that love of God and man which is the soul of the apostolate is communicated and nourished.[3]

Chautard's book has been recommended since the Council by Pope Paul VI, and by his immediate successor John Paul I in his first and only address to the priests of Rome. It is instructive to reread the work in the light of today's changed conditions of priestly life and work.

Jean Baptiste Chautard was born in 1858 at Briançon into a typical French family of that era: the father anticlerical, the mother a devout Catholic. Following the normal school education of the day, during which Jean Baptiste showed keen intelligence and great sensitivity, he was preparing for a business career in Marseilles, as desired by his father, when he underwent a religious conversion at age 17 which made him, for life, a man (in his biographer's words) "athirst for God."

Entering the Trappist monastery of Aiguebelle at age 19, over his father's embittered opposition, he passed through the normal monastic formation to priestly ordination in 1884. Thereafter he called the daily celebration of Mass the "center and sun"[4] of his whole day. Entrusted early with secretarial and administrative tasks in his community, he was elected Abbot of Chambarand in 1897, at age 39. His joy in this office (which he would later say belonged to his "golden age") was brief. After only two years he was elected Abbot of Sept-Fons in 1899—accepting this larger responsibility only after the personal intervention of Pope Leo XIII. He remained Abbot of Sept-Fons for the next thirty-six years, dying in the chapter house on September 29, 1935, just before giving the habit to a novice.

The book which would bring Chautard worldwide fame first appeared in 1907 as an aid to nuns engaged in catechetical work. To be successful, Chautard wrote, they must be both Mary and Martha, cultivating an intense inner life of prayer as the essential basis of an equally intense active apostolate.

Chautard embodied his central thesis in a revised version of the work published in 1909 with the title, *The Interior Life, the Basis of the Apostolate*. Revised and reissued in 1912 under the title by which it has been known ever since, the book achieved immediate success, passing through numerous editions, with many translations into other languages, and being recommended by successive Popes.

The work's central thesis, simply stated and often repeated, is the absolute necessity of a disciplined and regular life of prayer as the basis for any and all apostolic work. Lacking that, Chautard tells the reader, all active ministry is an exercise in futility.

Some of Chautard's examples seem strikingly modern, once allowance is made for the dated language and style. He quotes St. Alphonsus Liguori and St. Bernard of Clairvaux, for instance, to support his contention that if one does not look after one's own inner needs, one will be of no use to anyone. The same passage quotes a retreat note from Bishop Dupanloup: "I have recognized that *my want of interior life* is the source of all my troubles, of all my dryness, my weariness, my bad health" (43: emphasis in original). Clearly the Bishop of Orleans was experiencing what would today be called "burnout."

Equally modern is Chautard's emphasis on the primacy of liturgical over private prayer.

> The great prayer, the favorite channel of grace, is the *prayer of the Liturgy*, the prayer of the Church itself, *more powerful* than the prayer of individuals and even of pious associations, however powerful and commended in the Gospel prayer in solitude or prayer in common may be. (222)

Chautard also draws attention to the plural form of liturgical prayer, including the prayers of the Breviary, as an expression of the truth that "in the liturgy *everything is done in common, in the name of all, for the profit of all*" (224). He would surely have rejoiced in the *Constitution on the Sacred Liturgy* of Vatican II with its central affirmation: "The liturgy is the summit toward which the activity of the Church is directed: it is also the fount from which all her power flows" (SC 10).

Inevitably, however, there are passages in the book which seem dated today. A notable example is the lengthy description of "The Worker without the Interior Life" (77–90). This makes use of the "slippery slope" argument in terms which descend at times into bathos ("the angels of heaven weep": 81). The message itself is unexceptionable. For the contemporary reader, however, some of the language tends rather to risibility than to edification.

Jarring too is the unconcern with which Chautard refers in several places to "my Mass" (211, 248, 257)—as if the celebration of the Church's central mystery were a private priestly devotion. Clearly Chautard is simply following contemporary usage. He fails to note, however, that this language is difficult to reconcile with one of the book's central contentions: the corporate and public nature of the liturgy, even when it is celebrated privately.

A crucial section of the book, given its insistence on the indispensable need for prayer as the basis for all active work, is entitled "How shall I make my meditation?" (198–211). Chautard's answer is concerned entirely with discursive meditation: the active use of imagination, intellect, emotions, and will. He says nothing of the much older tradition of monastic prayer: the emptying of mind and imagination in order to enter into passive, silent contemplation, beyond all thoughts and images.

Only a few years after the appearance of Chautard's work, however, the Downside Benedictine Dom John Chapman, formed in the English

Benedictine tradition (far more "active" than that of the contemplative Trappists), was discovering that the methods of discursive meditation which Chautard prescribed for all engaged in the active apostolate soon led for most to tedium and the inability to meditate in this way at all. Chapman's *Spiritual Letters*[5] mark the beginning, at least for the English-speaking world, of the rediscovery of contemplative prayer which has come to wonderful fruition in our day in the writings of such authors as Thomas Merton, Thomas Keating, Basil Pennington, John Main, William Johnston and Laurence Freeman.

Chautard would surely have rejoiced in this recovery of one of the Church's greatest and most ancient treasures. Singly and in meditation groups the world over, tens of thousands of laypeople, priests, and religious of both sexes are finding spiritual nourishment in silent waiting upon God. So much is this so, in fact, that today "meditation" is generally understood to be not at all what Chautard meant by the word (discursive meditation), but rather what he would have called contemplation. In common with most spiritual writers of his era Chautard considered contemplation off-limits to all save a few specially "advanced souls." There is widespread agreement today that this restriction was an impoverishment.

By making simple forms of contemplative prayer available to all who are seriously trying to lead a life of Christian discipleship, today's spiritual guides are furthering the cause pleaded so passionately by the French Trappist at the beginning of this century in the categories, and with the arguments, of his day: the indispensability of regular, disciplined, personal prayer as the basis for all fruitful apostolic work.

Chautard's language and examples are often outmoded. His central message, however, is timeless—and in an activist age like our own more urgently necessary than ever.

* * *

Much the same could be said of another classic of priestly spirituality, almost completely neglected today: *The Eternal Priesthood* by the English convert-cardinal Henry Edward Manning.[6] The *bête noire* of his fellow convert John Henry Newman (whose own red hat Manning almost, but not quite, blocked by passing the word to Leo XIII that the mercurial Birmingham Oratorian had spurned it), Manning has had a bad press. This started soon after his death with his hostile first biographer Edmund Sheridan Purcell, who trashed his subject's reputation by consistently putting the worst interpretations on Manning's actions, reflections, and motives.

Purcell's destructive work was completed by Lytton Strachey, who chose Manning (after reading Purcell's *succes de scandale*) as the subject of the first and longest of the four biographical studies in his *Eminent Victorians*. The book, which more than all others established its author's literary reputation, is an extended exercise in witty and mocking exposure of Victorian over-earnestness and hypocrisy.

The great champion of papal infallibility at Vatican I, Manning was also a fearless campaigner for social justice long before Leo XIII's encyclical *Rerum novarum* (1891). Still without a definitive biography, Manning's tattered reputation has recently undergone rehabilitation at the hands of David Newsome in his brilliant double biography, *The Convert Cardinals*.[7]

In line with the prevailing textbook theology of his day Manning starts his best known work by defining priesthood in terms of the cultic powers conferred in ordination: "the twofold jurisdiction over the natural and the mystical Body of Christ—that is the power of consecration and the power of absolution" (1). In a later chapter, "The Priest as Preacher," Manning cites the statement of Trent that "preaching is the chief duty of bishops" (174) and adds that priests came to share this duty because of "the needs of the faithful" (175). Vatican II, by contrast, mentions preaching first among the offices conferred by priestly ordination.[8] Manning holds preaching in high esteem nonetheless. He takes his model from antiquity.

> They were then preachers, messengers, and evangelists. They were not pulpit orators…We cannot conceive these messengers of the kingdom of God laboring to compose their speech or studying the rules and graces of literary style. The records of their preaching in the New Testament are artless and simple as the growths of nature in a forest, which reveal the power and beauty of God. (175, 179)

Manning emphasizes the importance of preparation: of the sermon, but first of the preacher.

> It is the remote, not the proximate, preparation which is chiefly needed. The man preaches, not the sermon, and the sermon is as the man is (180).

Lest anyone suppose, however, that character could substitute for content, Manning stresses the need

> in boyhood to learn our mother-tongue...We ought also to learn early how to use our reason...Then in due time comes the knowledge of Holy Scripture, which explains the Catechism: and theology, which unfolds and develops [it] into the science of faith. These preparatory disciplines cannot be got up on occasion when wanted. They must have been wrought into the intelligence by a continuous and progressive formation. (182)

It would be a bold person indeed who claimed that these postulates are fulfilled today. Need our long-suffering laity look farther for an explanation of the low level of contemporary Catholic preaching?

Manning departs from the common Catholic teaching of his day—that only those who take religious vows are obliged to seek perfection, others having only the obligation to avoid sin—with the statement: "All are called to be Saints." He immediately qualifies this by adding: "not, indeed, in the same measure or degree" (52). Toward the end of the book, however, Manning says without qualification: "All Christians are called to be perfect, in whatsoever state of life" (280). Vatican II, in a notable rejection of the old double standard of morality, confirmed that Manning's statement alone is authentically Catholic:

> If, therefore, in the Church everyone does not proceed by the same path, nevertheless, all are called to sanctity and have received an equal privilege of faith through the justice of God. (LG 32)

The sanctity which Manning enjoins for all—but in special measure for priests as models for the flock they shepherd—consists not so much in the spiritual exercises which would figure so prominently in Chautard's work as in the faithful performance of daily duty. "Holiness consists not in doing uncommon things, but in doing all common things with an uncommon fervour" (81). Nor are fleshly sins the worst, Manning writes in another departure from the teaching prevalent in his day. Blackest of all are the sins

> of the spirit, such as the sins against charity, piety, and humility. The sin of Judas was, so far as is written, a spiritual sin...We are not safe from mortal sin by being only chaste and pure. (71)

In a day when Catholic seminarians were subject to discipline and regimentation which would be considered intolerable today, it was natural for Manning, in his chapter on "The Priest's Dangers," to compare the entry into priestly ministry to the launching of a ship. "When the stays are knocked away it goes down into the water, thence-forward to depend upon its own stability." That the transition remains difficult for many today is evident from the number of those who abandon priestly ministry in the early years—some, tragically, after only a few months.

Evidence that some things have indeed changed, however, is Manning's confident assertion:

> When the sun is down, the evening is the most precious part of a priest's day. It is the only time he can call his own. (131f)

Today's parish priest will read those sentences in shocked disbelief, wondering how there could ever have been a time when things were so different.

Though he enjoins daily mental prayer—listing this in his chapter on "The Priest's Helps" along with Mass, the Divine Office, preaching, and the guidance of souls in the confessional as "the five great sacerdotal graces" (105)—Manning gives no directions for meditation such as figure so largely in Chautard's work. A single phrase suggests, however, that Manning envisages something more akin to meditation in the sense in which the term is understood today: "the practice of mental prayer—that is, a life of contemplation" (105f).

In a passage which exemplifies the continuing importance of Manning's central message he calls prayer the greatest priestly help of all, and the most indispensable:

> There can be little doubt that the fertility of the lives of some pastors and the barrenness of others depend upon, and are measured by, their prayers. They who pray most will receive most; they who pray little will receive less...We are what we are before God, and nothing else, neither better nor worse. And we are what our communion with God makes us. Our faces shine, or are dim or darkened, as we are nearer or farther from God in prayer. A calm, recollected, joyous, hopeful mind is the reward of prayer. A restless, wandering, sad, and timid mind is the consequence of not praying as we ought. (128)

Such counsel is timeless. Every priest knows it in his heart. Those priests are happiest who never cease trying, despite repeated failure, to make Manning's words a reality in their lives.

Endnotes

1. Bernard Martelet (ed.), *L'âme de tout apostolat* (Editions St. Paul: Paris, 1979).

2. TAM Publications, Rockford, IL.

3. "*illa caritas erga Deum et homines, quae anima est totius apostolatus*" (LG 33). The force of the important "all" (in Chautard's title and this conciliar text) is impossible to reproduce in English translation.

4. *The Soul of the Apostolate* (Abbey of Gethsemane, 1946) p. 248. All subsequent citations are from this edition, with page numbers in parentheses in the text.

5. Published in 1935, the earliest letters were written during the First World War, only a few years after the first appearance of *L'âme de tout apostolat*.

6. The Newman Press, Westminster, MD: n.d. [1958?]. All citations are from this edition. Manning wrote the work, his most enduring literary production, in 1883.

7. John Murray: London, 1993. The book, by a layman in the Church of England, is an outstanding example of the biographer's art. Newsome successfully rehabilitates Manning without denigrating Newman.

8. "By the power of the sacrament of orders...[presbyters] are consecrated to preach the gospel and shepherd the faithful and to celebrate divine worship..." (LG 28). "Priests, as co-workers with their bishops, have the primary duty of proclaiming the gospel of God to all" (PO 4).

4

A New and Intense World of Ministry

Joseph A. Francis

Some twenty years ago, I attended a meeting of the Midwest Clergy Conference. This organization has as its purpose to bring together priests and religious whose ministries centered in African American Parishes. The organization has since ceased to exist and has been replaced by other organizations with the same purpose in mind. On one morning of the conference I walked into the coffee shop and was greeted by a rather rotund priest who called me by name even though I did not know who he was. He told me that his name was Father Gerety from New Haven, Connecticut. We parted without too much conversation. Several years later I heard that this priest had become the Bishop of Portland, Maine.

At the time I did not give this much thought, except to remark that the Diocese of Portland had been the See of the first African American Bishop in the United States, although Bishop Healy did not see himself in that light. Little did I know or dream that Bishop Gerety's life and mind would come together in a remarkable manner.

As I became known around the country by my association with the Conference of Major Superiors of Men, rumors began to spread that I was being "considered." One of my friends jokingly suggested that the Archdiocese of Newark would be a good place for me to have as my diocese. His tongue was really in his cheek.

Perhaps my friend was unknowingly prophetic. It seems that America was beginning to experience the inevitable. The Democracy on which we so prided ourselves was being looked upon in some amazing new ways. A new revolution was in the making and it caught so many by surprise. People were unprepared.

In the mid-sixties the great Black awareness revolution was in full bloom. Black activists called for reparations for past injustices to Black people. Black was no longer considered a term which designated inferiority, evil or the sinister. Racism was openly documented and denounced. Calls for equality in all phases of American life were loud and persistent. Christian Churches could no longer preach a gospel which promised true freedom from oppression as a reward to be handed out in the next life. The Catholic Church was not excluded from the condemnations.

During Easter Week of 1967, a group of Black priests met in Detroit in order to get to know one another and to hammer out an agenda that would place them at the very center of the Black Revolution in the Catholic Church in the United States. After almost twelve hours of debating and frustration, they issued a brief statement which accused the Catholic Church in the United States of blatant racism and called the Catholic Church in the United States "a white racist institution." Needless to say, this caused consternation at every level in the Church. The Black priests formed an organization and gave it the name of The National Black Catholic Clergy Caucus, a name by which it is still known today. I had the privilege of serving as its president in the seventies. Out of this organization was born the National Black Sisters Conference. Together the two conferences were responsible for the formation of the National Office for Black Catholics. This organization refused to come under the umbrella of the USCC, but challenged the USCC and the NCCB to respond to the needs of Black Catholics. The demand for funds was presented to the Bishops, who reacted negatively at first, but Archbishop Peter Leo Gerety carried the fight to the floor of the Conference and argued convincingly that the request of the NBCCC was legitimate, and for many reasons that would have an impact on the relationship of the Catholic Church to the Black Catholic Community. Archbishop Gerety called upon the twenty-five years he spent as the pastor of a Black Catholic Parish, St. Martin de Porres, in New Haven. He knew the Black Community and loved that Community and in turn was loved by that Black Community. Under the patronage of Archbishop Gerety and with the support of Cardinal Dearden, the National Office for Black Catholics flourished. I must add here that the National Black Catholic Clergy Caucus did not treat Archbishop Gerety with the kindness and gratitude which he deserved and deserves today.

I am certain that very few people in the Archdiocese of Newark, including priests, religious and laity, are aware of the role that Archbishop Gerety played in promoting the Catholic Social Agenda of the Church in the United States and abroad. He was one of the prime movers in the organization of the Campaign for Human Development and one of the principal architects of the Call to Action enterprise. The Call to Action provided a forum for the Church in the United States to really hear what the people of God had to say about their Church and what they wanted for the Church they loved. Those of us who were involved realized that much of what was said in the hearings were cries for deliverance, recognition and reconciliation. We also knew that many of the resolutions that would eventually come to the floor of the Conference would be non-negotiable, but having separated much of the wheat from the chaff, we responded. The pastoral letters on Racism, The Economy, War and Peace and even the failed pastoral on Women would not have been written had it not been for the Call to Action. However, even today there are many who shudder when the words are even mentioned.

When he became the Archbishop of Newark, he found himself surrounded by racial conflict and he recognized the role that Black anger and White racism played in the life of the City. He knew what he had to do and he made efforts to meet the challenge.

As I observed this giant of a man taking on the challenges of his time, it suddenly dawned on me that for so many years I had looked upon Bishops as aloof and distant individuals who by their very attire gave the impression that they could be approached by only a few, and that they might have been freed from the original sin of being essentially human like the rest of us. Even when I got to know a few Bishops rather well, I never heard them talk with affection about their parents or their relatives. I had almost come to the conclusion that Bishops were not allowed to talk about close relationships. I am sure now that these were misconceptions on my part. Archbishop Gerety changed all that for me. I even began to feel comfortable with Bishops. However, I knew with certainty that I would never be one of those titans that I had admired for so many years and for all the wrong reasons. I had to be about the business of trying to be a good priest and give my best to the persons and places to which I was called.

In 1975, I had the first of three major heart operations. I went into a period of discernment and decided that after my term as Provincial of the Southern Province of the Society of the Divine Word would end, I would bank the fires and spend the rest of my days in some small country parish in Louisiana. My final decision was made on Good Friday of

1976. On Holy Saturday morning I was informed that I had been named Auxiliary Bishop to Archbishop Gerety.

A few months after I had been ordained bishop, Archbishop Gerety called me and told me that he wanted to take me to New Haven. For a man who seemed to be so reserved at times, I was amazed at the outpouring of affection shown by the women, men and children of St. Martin de Porres Parish. The Archbishop relished every moment. At a special reception he had me dress in my episcopal splendor and then took me by the hand and said to the people: "Look at what I have brought to you, a genuine Black Bishop." By this gesture he wanted his people to know that it was possible for a Black man to become a Bishop in the Catholic Church, and in so doing he was assuring them that he had not forgotten them, who had been so much a part of his life as their pastor. I still go to New Haven on special occasions with the Archbishop and I bask with him in the great affection shown us.

As Archbishop Gerety's auxiliary, I entered a new and intense world of ministry. All of the dreams I had of how Vatican II should and would be implemented began to become a reality. At last I had found a Bishops' Bishop and a priests' Bishop, a people's Bishop whose only ambition was to make the Church of Newark come alive in the last quarter of the twentieth century. Ask most Auxiliary Bishops and they will tell you that their fate is worse than that of a Vice President of the United States. Not so with Archbishop Gerety. His Auxiliaries were intimate collaborators in the life of the Archdiocese. We were included in every major decision and the implementation of the policies and programs of the Archdiocese. It can be said that we were treated with dignity and respect. He was merely the first among equals.

I am compelled to relate here how Archbishop Gerety affirmed me during the time of one of my most tension-filled periods in the Bishops' Conference. Not long after I was ordained Bishop, I was asked to serve as a committee member of the Social Development and World Peace Committee. I had been very active in the Call to Action Program of the Bishops as we celebrated our bi-centennial year of the Country. Among the resolutions accepted by the Bishops was one that called for a pastoral letter on racism. At my very first meeting I was informed that I had been volunteered to chair the committee that would write the pastoral. Needless to say I was petrified. I came home and told Archbishop Gerety what had happened and he simply said, "Joe, you can do it."

It took almost two and a half years to complete the pastoral. Then came the day of reckoning. The Administrative Board of the NCCB/ USCC had approved the presentation of the pastoral to the Bishops in their November meeting of 1979. Only a committee Chairperson and his committee and staff can understand the feeling one has when they go before this formidable body of Ecclesiastics. When I arrived at the meeting, there was a lot scurrying around by the Chairperson of the Social Development and World Peace Committee. It seemed that a lot of people were saying that this pastoral on racism would never pass and rather than have the body of Bishops embarrassed by a negative vote, it might be better to table the pastoral for a more favorable time. I was called aside and asked to take the podium and remove the pastoral from the agenda. I refused, and indicated that the Chairperson of the larger committee would have to do this. I got a last minute reprieve and made my initial presentation to the Body. There were a few questions and some veiled comments, but no outright indication that the document would not be passed. In the meantime, Archbishop Gerety continued to encourage me. On the day of the vote, I had to face a barrage of questions and many objections, but somehow we were able to man the barricades and in the end we were rewarded with an overwhelming vote of approval. Archbishop Gerety came over and congratulated me and told me how proud he was of me. I still shiver when I think of myself on that podium. As I reflect now, I realize how much faith and courage the Archbishop had and that he had shared his faith in me and had given me the courage I needed.

In spite of a tremendous debt he inherited, Archbishop Gerety managed to keep ministry in the forefront of his priorities, while at the same time attempting to liquidate the huge debt, which he eventually did. The welfare of his flock was his top priority.

Archbishop Gerety took the documents of Vatican II very seriously. He studied them and, by bits and pieces, fitted them into the ministry of the Archdiocese. Many of his priests and some of his people did not move with the same kind of enthusiasm and some were even opposed to this new style of leadership. I suppose that they were afraid, a fear brought on by ignorance of what the Church is all about. The Archbishop was patient. He was very careful never to demand that priests and people comply; he preferred to refer to his recommendations as guidelines to be followed.

Programs like the "Father's Embrace" gave new hope to persons seeking reconciliation with the Church and with others. I have never been so moved as I was on the occasion of the first penance service, which, incidentally, was carried out according to the instructions of the Church. The RENEW Program was born in the Archdiocese of Newark, with the full support and encouragement of Archbishop Gerety. Instead of calling for a Synod, Archbishop Gerety launched an endeavor entitled "Fitting into the Future" which, in my opinion, surpassed anything that Synods are capable of doing. The program was not based on pre-conceived agendas, but was the product of intense and dedicated efforts of all the people of the Archdiocese. Sad to say, the whole program has been put to rest. Parishes and deaneries no longer speak of mission statements and goals and objectives. Those parishes that still do so are alive and well. The others survive on a maintenance model of operating only well enough to survive, but not grow in the life of the Spirit.

Archbishop Gerety never attempted to do it all with smoke and mirrors. He was open to criticism and even welcomed it. In my view, he was and remains today a true ecclesiastic, free of ambition. He may have disagreed with many persons in high places, but he never criticized them. He sought only to point out the positive elements of their ministry and character.

Archbishop Gerety is a man of deep spirituality. That spirituality is nurtured by prayer, reading and reflection on the deepest theological content of these times. I have often referred to him as "old school," as a pre-Vatican cleric whose foundation in faith and theology proved sturdy enough to sustain the massive construction of Vatican II. I happen to know too many who are afraid to build on their foundations of weak spirituality and weaker theology and there are those who have tried to build without any foundation at all.

As I look back now, I miss those intense dialogues, conversations and even confrontations that took place in his study, on his sailboat, in restaurants and even as we relaxed on vacation. Good conversations and exchanges are the stuff that engender mutual respect.

The Gerety years have helped me to grow in so many ways. The affirmation he gave me and still gives me has kept me from becoming a frustrated, bitter individual. For all that he has done with me and for me, I am grateful. As I pointed out earlier, he is my friend and for that I love him. He has fitted my life and the lives of thousands into a future of hope and assurance. Archbishop Peter Leo Gerety will be seen as a modern day prophet by all who know him. He is a great priest. Sacerdos Magnus, qui in diebus ejus placuit Deum!

5

The Passionateness of Being: A Meditation

Richard M. Liddy

In an article dedicated to for Edward Schillebeeckx in 1976 Bernard Lonergan referred to "the passionateness of being."[1]

What possibly could he have meant by such a phrase? After all, for the most part one thinks of "being" as a cold, lifeless, philosophical concept. It reminds one of an old and outdated metaphysics. What could "being" have to do with passion?—with desire?—with a desire so intense one would suffer for it?

In this short article, a tribute to Archbishop Peter Leo Gerety, I would like to reflect on this phrase and its meaning. My topics are:

1) Being;
2) Beyond Appearances;
3) Saints and Scholars;
4) Education.

In all of this I am profoundly indebted to the thought and writings of Bernard Lonergan. My aim is to link a philosophical term to the desires of the human heart, much as Paul did on the Areopagus:

> As I walked around looking at your shrines, I even discovered an altar inscribed, "To a God Unknown." Now, what you are thus worshiping in ignorance I intend to make known to you. (Acts 17:23)

1) BEING

When Lonergan uses the term, being, the last thing he is referring to is an abstract concept. In fact, what he is referring to is totally concrete:

in fact, it is everything about everything. It includes the universe, ourselves and everything else.

But how do we get a handle on being, on "everything about everything?"

Only by asking and answering questions. By the child's incessant "What is this, Mommy?" and "What is that?" And by the insights and correct judgments the child makes as he or she "grows up." And by the scientist's careful and methodical questioning as he penetrates into the secrets of the universe. And by the lover's questions of her beloved as she seeks to get to know him on deeper and deeper levels. And by the religious person's question, "Who **is** this God who has captured my heart?"

Being, then, is the object of our "pure desire to know." It is what we know already and what remains yet to be known. The search for being begins in wonder, and wonder, as Kierkegaard noted, is not unconnected to worship.

> ...the expression of wonder is worship. And wonder is an ambiguous state of mind which comprises fear and bliss. Worship therefore is mingled fear and bliss all at once.[2]

In seeking being we are impelled by what Lonergan calls "the notion of being" that is written into our minds and hearts. This is the dynamic anticipation of our spirit that seeks to understand this or that realm of being, but ultimately, if open, seeks to know everything about everything.

Such a notion of being has political implications. No state can rightfully rule questioning out of bounds—as has taken place in our own century. Nor can other, more subtle, political and social pressures rightfully inhibit us from questioning.

Such a notion of being, faced with our human experience, seeks acts of understanding and correct judgments in this or that realm. The farmer develops a refined sense of the weather patterns; and a star athlete grasps more finely the possibilities of his sport; and a theologian comes to understand ever more fully the sources and implications of revelation. But if we are not to be obscurantists, we will not stifle the further questions. We will seek to get beyond ourselves—where we are now; we will seek to transcend ourselves by always raising the further question and by seeking to answer such questions by understanding and true judgment.

Such is being: it is not primarily a concept; it is whatever draws us to intelligibility in any area and to the intelligibility of the whole of things: to truth, to reality, to goodness, to love.

Being is the notion of what we are all created to seek.

2) BEYOND APPEARANCES

One of the major characteristics of the notion of being is that it is a call heard within our own very spirits; and, if we listen, it is a call to move beyond appearances. The notion of being is a call to move beyond what seems to be to what is. It is also a call to move beyond what merely "feels good" to what is good. Once we arrive at what is true and good in any area, the die is cast; our very being calls us to move in that direction.

The questioning that is at the core of the notion of being moves us beyond materialism in any of its guises, beyond my accepted common sense world, beyond pragmatic criteria, to the higher viewpoint, the long-range viewpoint, the world of true meanings and values.

The notion of being heads us beyond money and power to ask, "Is that all there is?" "Is this quest I am on really good?" "What am I really being called to?" "What is my vocation, my 'call'?"

Thus, in the newspaper this morning Elie Wiesel is quoted about his reluctance to make videos: "I don't trust images—I trust words," he said. Words move us beyond the MTV image world—they can introduce us to being.

The notion of being heads us beyond drifting to ask, "What's worthwhile?" "What's truly worth my while?" "What's worth loving?" "What's worth giving my body for?" "What's worth giving my life for?" "What's worth dying for?"

Thus, intimations of the passionateness of being.

It is truly a **radical** notion; for it comes from our roots. It comes from the heart of our own being and it is capable of asking everything about everything. It moves us from enthusiasms and bandwagons to understanding and truth; from the merely satisfying to the truly valuable; from selfishness to self-giving love.

As Christians, we can believe that God has written the notion of being into our very being. That notion gets us out of ourselves in the self-transcending acts of questioning, understanding, judging, evaluating, deciding, acting, loving. And if it is true that God has indeed already given himself to us, then it is also true that our deepest being, constituted by the passionate notion of being, cannot truly find fulfillment outside of self-emptying love. The very being of the human person is not static but dynamic; it never is a state of achieved perfection; it always is at best a striving. And "the striving of the religious man is to give himself to God in something nearer the way in which God has given himself to us."[3]

Indeed, the notion of being can make it possible for every day to be worth living. Notice how the notion of being, the openness of our spirits to the absolute fullness of love, is implicit in the following quote from Father Pedro Arrupe, S.J.:

Nothing is more practical than finding God, that is, than falling in love in a quite absolute, final way. What you are in love with, what seizes your imagination, will affect everything. It will decide

— what will get you out of bed in the morning,
— what you will do with your evenings,
— how you spend your weekends,
— what you read,
— who you know,
— what breaks your heart,
— and what amazes you with joy and gratitude.

Fall in love, stay in love, and it will decide everything.

3) SAINTS AND SCHOLARS

Lonergan writes of "the passionateness of being" in the context of evolutionary world process. Somehow, in some way, the billions of years old universe with its countless elements and teeming physical, chemical and biological processes—somehow this whole incalculable mass and momentum has arrived at: ourselves.

Evolutionary process has arrived at conscious persons who can wonder at and catch glimmers of this eon-old process. In our minds the universe can become "luminous"; and we can wonder at our own power to wonder and to bring to light these wonderful dimensions of the universe. And we can wonder about a Mind beyond our minds and beyond the universe; and about an absolute Truth beyond the limited truths we know; and about a Goodness beyond ourselves and the world.

And we can be open to knowing and loving.

Even human sexuality is encompassed by the upward thrust of the finality of all being.

> The sexual extravagance of man, unparalleled in the animals, has its ultimate ground in St. Augustine's "Thou has made us for thyself, O Lord, and our hearts are restless till they rest in thee."[4]

In an article from the early 1940's Lonergan expressed "the passionateness of being" by understanding the organistic drives of nature itself as related to human friendship and ultimately to self-sacrificing love.

> Now towards this high goal of charity it is no small beginning in the weak and imperfect heart of fallen man to be startled by a beauty that shifts the center of appetition out of self; and such a shift is effected on the level of sensitive spontaneity by **Eros** leaping in [and] through delighted eyes and establishing itself as unrest in absence and in imperious demand for company. Next company may reveal deeper qualities of mind and character to shift again the center from the merely organistic tendencies of nature to the rational level of friendship with its enduring basis in the excellence of a good person. Finally, grace inserts into charity the love that nature gives and reason approves.[5]

And saints and saintly people are those who have fallen in love with this One—this One who Christians believe has poured his own mysterious love into our hearts: the Spirit of the Father whom Jesus died to send us.

Somehow the saints "got it." They "got" the passionateness of being. From all the intimations in the world around them, they got it; and so they risked their lives in love. A Francis of Assisi, a Teresa of Avila—these were extremely passionate people. And in our own day we have the example of those who gave their lives because they were passionate about the object their spirits were seeking: a Dorothy Day, and Oscar Romero.

And scholars—what about scholars? The day to day plugging. Searching out one false lead after another. In the face of discouragement, hoping against hope. Hidden in libraries and studies, plunging each day beyond the apparent; each day moving beyond the material; beyond power; driven only by the desire to know, the love of the truth, the notion of being.

Are these not also caught up in the passionateness of being? Are these not also caught up—as the saying goes—"in the throe of wonder"?[6]

Lonergan was once asked about action on behalf of the poor, and he gave a most interesting answer.

Cardinal Danielou speaks of the poor. It is a worthy topic, but I feel that the basic step in aiding them in a notable manner is a matter of spending one's nights and days in a deep and prolonged study of economic analysis.[7]

4) EDUCATION

The passionateness of being has implications for education. For besides information there is formation. And besides formation there is transformation.

Formation, the disciplines and structures of education, goes far beyond the imparting of information. But transformation is the goal of all education, all formation. And such transformation only takes place through the personal heeding, and faithfulness to, the notion of being.

Transformation takes place through fidelity to the questioning, reflecting and evaluating which are expressions of the notion of being. Transformation takes place through leaving behind the image world of appearances, through honesty and humility, through following "love's way," the way of the Holy Spirit. All this requires another type of education than the mere imparting of information. It implies an attentiveness to—and helping others to be attentive to—the signs of the Spirit, the signs of love.

> In a manner of speaking, we are falling in love at every turn of the road, with a fold in the hills, the mist over the lake, the stars tangled in the bare branches, the yellow chair in the sunlight, an old song at the peasant's fireside, a new thought flashing from the pages of a book, a lined face on a hospital pillow, a hair ribbon from Ur of the Chaldees.[8]

Saint Ignatius of Loyola developed his **Spiritual Exercises** in order to help people discern the movements of the Holy Spirit in their own souls, in the "consolations and desolation" of their own hearts. Today, some have developed Ignatius' method through the daily **"examen"** that focuses on the experiences, feeling and decisions of daily living.

One "rummages" in one's memories and feelings and encounters with persons for the hints of the Spirit, the "consolation without a cause" that Ignatius felt was the sign of the Spirit's presence beckoning us to new life.[9]

And in a sort of **praeparatio evangelica**, Abraham Maslow wrote of this new type of education in which people are asked to be attentive to their own "peak experiences" that call them out of themselves in their own self-transcendence toward being.

> All this implies another kind of education, i.e., experiential educa-tion...it also implies another kind of communication...What we are implying is that...what is necessary to do first is to change the person and to change his awareness of himself. That is, we must make him aware of the fact that peak-experiences go on inside himself. Until he has become aware of such experience and has this experience as the basis for a comparison, he is non-peaker; and it is useless to try to com-municate to him the feel and the nature of peak-experience. But if we can change him, in the sense of making him aware of what is going on inside himself, then he becomes a different kind of communicatee. He now knows that what you are talking about when you speak of peak-experiences; and it is possible to teach him by reference to his own weak peak-experiences how to improve them, how to enrich them, how to enlarge them, and also how to draw the proper conclusions from them...

> ...In all of these we may use the paradigm that the process of education (and of therapy) is helping the person to become aware of internal, sub-jective, subverbal experiences so that these experiences can be brought into the world of abstraction, of conversation, of communication, of naming, etc., with the consequence that it immediately becomes possi-ble for a certain amount of control to be exerted over these hitherto unconscious and uncontrollable processes.[10]

This is, of course, Bernard Lonergan's whole program: a self-appro-priation that involves recognizing within oneself the passionateness of the notion of being that calls one out of oneself to intelligibility, to truth, to falling in love with Love.

The passionateness of being is what Jesus came to teach us: that lay-ing down one's life for being, for the true, the good, for others, for God, is indeed that for which we were created.

Endnotes

1. Bernard Lonergan, "Mission and the Spirit," *A Third Collection* (New York: 1985), 29.

2. Søren Kierkegaard, "Three Discourses on Imagined Occasions."

3. Bernard Lonergan, *A Second Collection* (Philadelphia: The Westminster Press, 1974), 147.

4. Bernard Lonergan, "Finality, Love, Marriage," *Collection* (Toronto: University of Toronto Press, 1988), 49.

5. Ibid., 31–32.

6. Cf. Jerome A. Miller, *In the Throe of Wonder* (Albany, NY: State University of New York Press, 1992).

7. Bernard Lonergan, "Sacralization and Secularization," 1973, unpublished.

8. John V. Taylor, *The Go-Between God* (Philadelphia: Fortress Press, 1973), 9.

9. Cf. Dennis Hamm, "Rummaging for God: Praying Backward Through Your Day," *America*, May 14, 1994, 22–23.

10. Abraham Maslow, *Religions, Values, and Peak Experiences* (New York: Viking Press, 1970), 89f.

6

Dear Archbishop

Doris Hudson

Dear Archbishop Gerety,

When the letter from Father Cassian arrived in mid-September requesting my participation in this tribute, I was still overwhelmed by the painful and devastating loss of Al only a month before. For the longest time I did not respond although this exciting project was in my thoughts constantly. I could focus on neither topic nor method. Changes in the lives of my family and the decisions which faced me further complicated my life. I wrote to Father explaining this mental, emotional and spiritual bloc but he persuaded me to be patient because there was still time to collect my thoughts.

Months later as the deadline neared I became more distressed because I was still unable to get on task. After a very long absence from active Church ministry, I was out of practice and away from the spiritual well of reading and participation which had fueled the writing and speaking talents which God had given to me. My main concern was your not understanding why I had not been able to participate, although further reflection assured me that would be uncharacteristic of you.

Then the Lord took pity on me. In the stillness of the night He reminded me that you and I had exchanged letters for twenty years about many serious and not so serious topics. So why not write this tribute to you in the simple, informal, letter style with which I am most comfortable at this time. I will try not to think too much about the fact that others can read these as well, and that for me, a private person in my relationships, that is a very real sacrifice.

These thoughts, expressed spontaneously in letter form, will be from the heart and mind of one who, with Al, has respected and loved you as a priest and friend for twenty years. I will write to you about anything that moves me in the next week. Now it will be fun!

Love and peace,
Doris

Dear Archbishop Gerety,

One of the reasons we have communicated so frequently with letters is that you always responded thoughtfully and promptly, even to letters in which I lamented the Church's actions or lack thereof. Your patience was extraordinary, and when I seemed too distressed your advice was to "go to a movie with Al or run around the block." (Occasionally I even followed your suggestion. After all it was, you said, the advice given to you many years ago by a wise mentor.)

Your consideration of new ideas, readings and projects presented to you by me and others was frequently followed by meetings and action. I and others were taken seriously in our efforts to help continue the renewal of the Church in Newark and beyond.

It was exhilarating being active in Church renewal in the 60's and 70's. Even before Vatican II, Al and I were reading and discussing with others possible changes that might be considered. When Vatican II occurred we were ecstatic and for the next fifteen years, on the parish, diocesan and national levels, we were involved in the emerging Vatican II Church.

This period was not without frustration and discouragement. Mistakes were made, the process was slow and sometimes incompetent. Dissension grew among us about the direction, methods and substance of new programs, roles, the development of new forms of community and shared responsibility. Unfortunately, this is more common than not with change makers. New ideas and new ways are often diverse while those who support the status quo are united in their opposition.

As we continued our efforts to change or redefine traditions and roles, there was increased reaction from many different sources, overtly and covertly. There were those in the Church who wanted little or no change, who did not approve of Vatican II or who saw our activities as unnecessary, unwanted and even evil. I have often thought of the words of an activist whose name I can't recall and I paraphrase them here: Whenever the forces for good begin to make progress, from out of nowhere emerges powerful and often vicious opposition. In 1974, discouraged by these reactions and obstacles, Al and I considered making a change in our commitments.

Then we heard some good news. A new Bishop was coming to town. The advance reports were good: his written reaction to Vietnam, shared responsibility in Maine, his ministry for and with minorities, enthusiastic support for Vatican II, the owner of a sailboat that was not the newest and grandest in Casco Bay (I heard this last item from Kevin Concannon who was serving on the National Bishops' Advisory Council with me and who was from the Portland Diocese). Last but not least, we heard the new Archbishop had ordered a Ford as his official automobile. Al and I decided to stay and work with this new leader.

As a member of the Archdiocesan Pastoral Council I shook your hand (I was never into kissing rings) and wished you Godspeed at your installation. I remember also that it poured rain that evening, but nothing could dampen our spirits. We were ready once again to meet, pray, dream and plan for the future. You did not disappoint us.

Thank you for the faith, hope and wonderful attitude which you brought with you.

Love and peace,
Doris

Dear Archbishop Gerety,

The first time we had a conversation was in 1975 after a parish council committee meeting in Sacred Heart Cathedral Rectory. I had been recently elected to the National Bishops' Advisory Council and you wished to discuss it with me. What I remember most about that initial meeting, however, was your telling me that you were a parish priest at heart and you wanted me to relate to you that way. That was fine with me since I was never particularly impressed with the trappings of Church royalty or any other kind for that matter. (I would have loved to have been a part of our founding fathers' group, as a mother, of course, when they fashioned the early documents of that daring experiment called democracy. There were mandates about bowing to royalty and accepting royal titles.)

Now parish priests have always been near and dear to the hearts of Al and me. Many times we reflected on their influence in our lives and their commitment to us of time, talent and inspiration. As Al and I were reminiscing during our last months together he would frequently refer to priests, past and present, who were special in his life. We both considered the parish the heart of the Church and we wondered together how fewer priests and sisters serving larger numbers would affect our adult children, their spouses and our four grandsons. What and who will minister to them, call them to spiritual growth and community and remind them at least once a week about their priestly role in their worlds?

It is a time when we need radical changes in ministry, roles and community structures in order to move the Church into the twenty-first century. We need to respond to the searching and yearning of people of all ages for more meaningful and smaller communities where spiritual growth and development can help them to live Christian lives in their very complex world. There seems to be little activity or discussion about these changes which are inevitable if the needs of the faithful are to be met.

We have learned much about the mistakes we made in how we implemented Vatican II. Among them was our inattention to the diversity of cultures in the world. This diversity demands a decentralized plan which is tailored to the lives and needs of people where they are in life style, location and spirituality. We need to move forward with sensitivity, love and faith using the many gifts of all our people. We need also to learn to work better with people of different beliefs, emphasizing how we are alike rather than how we are different. Most people of good will share a common vision of creating a better world for our posterity.

Centuries ago the world changed slowly and we could afford to be patient and reflective. Now we in the Western world cannot keep pace with the accelerating changes which are all about us. The leadership of the Church must be dynamic, creative and fearless in planning for the future. Above all, the leaders must be in touch with the grass roots Church. Please God, may such leaders arise and, along with Christian people and others who are willing to devote time, talent, and resources, prepare as quickly as possible for tomorrow.

I know elsewhere in this publication there are stories about your twenty year ministry as a parish priest. I will, therefore, only comment briefly on the time you took Al and me to visit St. Martin de Porres Church to show us where those wonderful years were experienced. That visit was enjoyable and reinforced our respect for your grass roots pastoral ministry and the knowledge that you were a man ahead of his time.

Enough nostalgia for one night, you say. I agree. Until the Fourth Epistle,

Love and peace,
Doris

Dear Archbishop Gerety,

As you know, one of my favorite topics is the adventures of my six year old grandson Sean who has Down Syndrome. There has never been a dull moment in his life and the lives of those who form his circle of life and love. Recently the little newsletter which is mailed to interested families in the area by a group of parents of Down Syndrome children included a piece which they requested me to write as Sean's grandma. I include this here as an introduction to more information on Sean and as a remembrance of the great love shared by Al and Sean. When Al died, Father Gusmer, who had brought communion to Al every week and, near the end, every few days, suggested that we tell our four little, very upset grandsons that Grandpa had a special star in the heavens which would be his light for them to look for when they felt sad.

- When our first grandchild arrived Al and I were to set out on still another adventure, one filled with love, challenge and surprise. The surprise was Sean, a beautiful baby who captured our hearts, our attention and our time in not only the usual ways, but in many unusual ones as well. These next lines are about one small part of that adventure entitled "Sean and His Grandpa."

- To his Grandpa, Sean was the "apple of his eye." Cradled in his arms and held later on his broad shoulders, Sean was walked all over Verona, into nearby parks and onto faraway beaches where he was treated to the sounds and sights of birds, squirrels, the sky, the sun, moon and stars, the sand and the ocean and every wonder, natural and man-made. On these same broad shoulders, Sean was carried to open heart surgery at the tender age of seven months. All this before the age of one!

- Grandpa was never too busy to interrupt his work day to observe Sean at school. At Stepping Stones he was a frequent visitor, and because Sean always wanted to go to him, his Grandpa had to be content to watch him from a distance. Later, Grandpa was a sure presence at Grandparents' Day at Verona Preschool where Sean's progress would never fail to delight and amaze him.

- In this past year as his Grandpa became very ill, Sean, never shy or nervous, would visit him daily. He would bound in with a big smile and a "Hi, Grandpa," disappointed only because he could no longer be cradled in those loving arms. His Grandpa always responded with a smile and an extended hand, which he held for a moment.

• Now Sean walks with his Grandma in the evening and looks up in the heavens for Grandpa's star, assured that he is still watching him and that someday again they will walk together to experience together the wonders of still another place.

In the next letter I will write more on Sean and one of the innovations in the education of children with disabilities called Inclusion. When I retire from teaching in June, this and other related areas will be one major involvement for me.

Love and peace,
Doris

Dear Archbishop Gerety,

Inclusion—what a wonderful Christian word! Jesus included everyone in His life and through His death by redeeming us. For those whom many excluded from their lives because they considered them unworthy, inferior, immoral or socially unacceptable, He performed miracles, broke bread, healed them in mind, body, and spirit and even on occasion held them up as examples for the self-righteous to emulate. Prostitutes and thieves, tax collectors and foreigners, pagans and illiterates, the sick and the poor, all were welcomed into Christ's circle of love and redeemed by His sacrifice on the cross.

Today, we are becoming painfully aware of all the groups we exclude for one reason or another: the homeless, the elderly, women, immigrants, homosexuals, minorities—racial, religious and ethnic— the jobless, the disabled and many others. They have been segregated in their communities, schools, churches, recreation facilities and employment.

One of these groups, the disabled, has become the focus of my attention because of Sean. I had never really thought much about the fact that most of these children have been out of sight for a very long time. In the past, many were institutionalized or hidden in homes, sometimes on the advice of doctors or family members who considered them a punishment and a source of embarrassment. This accounts for the fact that most of us have been uncomfortable when we encounter these people and relate to them only briefly and sometimes avoid them altogether.

Recently, across the country there has been an educational movement called Inclusion. Its purpose is to keep these children in their own communities where they rightfully belong. Children with disabilities, mental or physical, should be attending local schools and be placed in regular classrooms with the supportive assistance which is needed. How awful to have segregated these children from the rest of their peers in their neighborhoods, schools and churches.

When Sean was three, Celeste tried to enroll him in a Catholic preschool program. He was turned down without an interview or an evaluation because the teachers could not "handle" a child of this type and he would interfere with the activities of the other "normal" children. Fortunately, in a nearby parish, he was welcomed with open arms and has been with his peers ever since.

Many parishes still prepare disabled children for the reception of the sacraments in special classes apart from the others. Again, some parishes at the urging of parents now include these children with their friends and neighbors.

What do they have to give to us? What we need most: kindness, love, warmth, affection, concern, companionship. Many of them are humorous, delightful children, quick to forgive and capable of learning, working and playing on many levels. Sean does not have mean genes. He can show us what it is to be truly human and Christ-like. Maybe we are the ones who are not "normal" as God the Creator intended.

When I wrote to you, Archbishop, about Sean's birth your response was immediate and I quote it in part: "As I have learned over many years of involvement in such matters these little children can be a source of joy and comfort to their parents." And to everyone else who is lucky enough to know and love them.

One of your Inclusion programs on which I worked and which I loved was "The Father's Embrace," a call to the whole diocese to repent and reconcile. It was a huge success. Efforts like this are rare today. Do rules and regulations interfere with the Gospel?

Inclusion, love, Gospel, Jesus. Thank you for including me in the efforts of the Church of Newark to include others. Pray for our small beginnings in trying to enable all little children to really belong.

Love and peace,
Doris

Dear Archbishop Gerety,

You have only one more letter to read. This one publicly thanks you for the kindness and love you shared with Al during the last several years of his life. As I have told you privately, our visits with you, the celebration of the Eucharist, your visits to him when he could no longer go out helped us to cope with his terminal illness. You read Scripture, prayed with and over Al, and spoke thoughtful and inspiring words to him. Always your message was filled with the hope, optimism and faith which are so much a part of you. Your good humor and stories brought a smile to our faces and hearts.

The funeral liturgy celebrated by you and other priests who have been part of our lives raised the spirits of our family and friends. The children and I were overwhelmed by our great loss to the point where we did not think we could take part in the liturgy and maintain control. Miracles of healing occurred during that Eucharist and each of us left the church with a deep feeling of peace. It will forever remind us of how the liturgy should be celebrated and how death can be celebrated as well as life. We are forever grateful to all those who participated and supported us during those difficult days.

I will miss Al every day of my life for he was my oldest and dearest friend, the love of my life, the father of my children and a Christ filled role model to us all. I know you understand that was the reason I had such difficulty initially focusing on these writings.

I could go on, but I know you are breathing a sigh of relief because I am at the end—for now anyway. I will close wishing you the traditional Irish Blessing which was on Al's remembrance card:

May the road rise to meet you.
May the wind be always at your back.
May the sun shine warm upon your face,
The rain fall soft upon your fields.
And until we meet again,
May God hold you in the palm of His hand.

Amen.

Love and peace,
Doris

7

A Pastoral Vision

Thomas P. Ivory

After serving as Spiritual Director at The American College at the University of Louvain, Belgium for five years, I returned to my home Archdiocese of Newark in 1974 to welcome our new Archbishop Peter L. Gerety. His pastoral style and reputation as Bishop in the Diocese of Portland, Maine and in his inner-city parish ministry in New Haven, Connecticut, had brought a certain level of excitement and anticipation to the pastoral leaders in Newark. One of our priests joked with him at a meeting of our Senate of Priests: "Your appointment to Newark was like attaching a jet engine to a trolley car!"

In the mid 1970's the Newark Archdiocese, located in the northeast urbanized corner of New Jersey, was facing an enormous diocesan debt of $40 million as well as the various problems and challenges raised by new immigrants, racial and ethnic tensions, ideological extremists within the Church, and the new understanding of the roles of laity and clergy raised by the Second Vatican Council. In the midst of what might be considered as a microcosm of the Church in the United States at that period of time, Archbishop Gerety brought a high level of pastoral and theological acumen to his key leadership role. His primary concern was spiritual renewal, and he encouraged creativity and subsidiarity through his ability to delegate responsibilities. One of his more famous quotations was: "Don't just bring me problems, but solutions!"

Equally impressive was Archbishop Gerety's sense of the universal mission in the Church. His breadth of vision was demonstrated by his openness in sharing his resource personnel to assist other dioceses or apostolates in various parts of the world. Laypersons and priests were encouraged to use their talents wherever they could be helpful for the mission of Jesus Christ.

Other authors will write from their perspectives, and so it is hoped that the articles of this Festschrift will illuminate numerous facets of the life and ministry of Archbishop Gerety. My purpose in this article is to focus on how he allowed the pastoral vision offered by the restored Order of Christian Initiation of Adults to take form and become implemented in the life of our Church in the Newark Archdiocese. As Archdiocesan Director of Religious Education between 1975 and 1985, I was privileged to assist in that process and to benefit from his pastoral leadership. We will reflect on five developments which flowed from this pastoral vision: Confirmation Guidelines, RENEW, Baptismal Guidelines, Ministerial Development Center, and the Archdiocesan Pastoral Direction.

CONFIRMATION GUIDELINES

The celebration of the Sacrament of Confirmation continues to be a pastoral challenge in the mid 1990's, just as it was in the mid 1970's when Archbishop Gerety approved the appointment of a joint committee (from both his catechetical and liturgical offices) to prepare a draft of Guidelines for Confirmation. The Adult Catechumenate served as the standard, not only for the catechesis of unbaptized adults, but also as a model for the catechesis of baptized adults and youth preparing for full sacramental initiation. In his letter of promulgation, April 1, 1979, Archbishop Gerety wrote:

> As the new Rite of Christian Initiation of Adults reminds us, Confirmation is one of the sacraments of initiation. The preface of the Archdiocesan Guidelines calls for catechetical programs for Confirmation to help the candidate to become more fully aware of the meaning and implications of initiation into the life of the Christian community. Furthermore, this celebration of Christian initiation should be seen as an experience of the entire community at prayer, welcoming the candidates into fuller communion, and inviting them to continue their lifelong spiritual growth within and along with the community of faith.

The Preface to which Archbishop Gerety refers articulates this vision more fully:

The process of initiation into the Catholic Church involves three sacramental events: Baptism, Confirmation and Eucharist. Although the pastoral practice of celebrating these sacraments has varied in different ages and rites, it currently consists in celebrating them separately. These three sacraments should be viewed together in a common theological context of conversion and initiation. Confirmation seals the Baptismal event, and Eucharist is the on-going celebration of participation in the Paschal Mystery. As the word itself implies, Confirmation is a personalized affirmation of Baptism, a determination to strive to live in the spirit of the Gospel values. Such a commitment, sacramentalized in Confirmation, needs to be further interiorized and constantly renewed in Christian adulthood.

Catechetical programs for the sacrament of Confirmation should help the candidate to become more fully aware of the meaning and implications of initiation into the life of the Christian Community. Confirmation catechesis should be related to the preparation programs and celebration of Baptism and Eucharist so as to express effectively the on-going process of Christian Initiation. The catechesis ought to be multi-dimensional, that is, it ought to develop the doctrinal, liturgical, communal and apostolic dimensions of this sacrament. Confirmation should be celebrated as a sign of what the candidate is experiencing in the local faith community and is witnessing in his or her personal life style. This celebration of Christian initiation should be seen as an experience of the entire community at prayer, welcoming the candidates into fuller communion and inviting them to continue their lifelong spiritual growth within and along the community of faith. The prayerful nature of the Sacrament of Confirmation should be clearly maintained in both the catechesis and in the planning for the liturgical celebration. Since most Catholics have been baptized as infants, the initiation process necessarily extends for a number of years. To manifest this continuity requires a great deal of planning and coordination in developing parish initiation programs.

The catechumenal model can be seen in the emphasis which the Guidelines place on the parish community which is completing the initiation of its members in Confirmation. Before speaking of the actual candidates, the Guidelines enunciate the responsibilities of the parish community, the sponsors and parents, the Confirmation team and the catechists. The following paragraphs from the Guidelines will demonstrate the catechumenal vision for the renewal of parishes celebrating Confirmation:

Parish Community

23. The parish community must be conscious that it represents the Church for the young person and that initiation of new members should be the concern and business of all the baptized. Accordingly, it should review and renew its spirit and life as a faith community. As the candidates freely discern their coming to faith and conversion within the Catholic Church, so also the parish should prayerfully discern:

• its spirit of renewal
• its quality of faith
• its willingness to enter into the on-going process of conversion called for in the Gospel, and
• its willingness communally to guide, to catechize and prayerfully to support these candidates.

24. As a central goal of the catechesis the parish should encourage a growing sense of respect for the active presence of the Holy Spirit within the life of the community and its individual members. Parish preparation programs then should strive to involve the entire parish community so that this life and its gifts may be manifest to the candidates.

25. By a vibrant communal celebration of this Sacrament, with the Archbishop or his assistant bishops present as the spiritual leaders of the local diocesan Church, the parish reaffirms its efforts for continued renewal.

26. Conscious of her nature as a pilgrim, the local Church will offer varied multi-dimensional programs of continuing education, respectful of the different levels of readiness and growth in individuals. The parish community should assist the confirmed Catholic in his or her lifelong response to the Gospel of Jesus Christ through opportunities which respond to the needs of the parish and the broader community.

Regarding the age of the youth candidates for Confirmation, the Newark Guidelines provided a masterful understatement, which is still the situation a generation later:

31. The age of Confirmation is a question of common concern, but one which cannot be definitely settled at the present time. Much more study of the whole process of Christian Initiation is necessary, and the type of faith community into which a person is being initiated must be examined. The introduction to the *Rite of Confirmation* (n.11) gives preference to the traditional order of Baptism, Confirmation and First

Eucharist, but for pastoral reasons, Confirmation may be postponed until a more mature age is reached. With due respect for the varying rate of individual growth in maturity, ages will vary. The evaluative criteria listed above suggest a certain measure of mature awareness of the meaning of the Christian way of life and personal determination to become a more vibrant and responsible member of the Christian community.

Some indicators were provided for evaluating the readiness of candidates in paragraph 30:

- a recognition by the young person that he or she is a unique person with various gifts to offer
- a willingness expressed by the young person to share his or her gifts with the many communities of which he or she is a part
- a willingness to live in the spirit of his or her Baptism by openness to growth and service
- an adequate grasp of the content of the Catholic faith experience
- an ability of the young person freely to request the Sacrament of Confirmation and to give his or her reasons for doing so
- a willingness to be involved in the communal and apostolic aspects of the program
- an appreciation expressed by the young person for the empowering assistance of the Holy Spirit in his or her life and in the life of the community.

Although Archbishop Gerety was reluctant to set a minimum age for youth candidates for Confirmation, the Guidelines called for a period of remote preparation which would include the total elementary and junior high religious education programs containing a presentation of the basic articles of faith. A period of immediate preparation was to take place within the context of a parish youth ministry thrust, and included meaningful experiences of Christian communal living, expressed in service projects, retreat weekends and parish liturgies.

At one point in the preliminary committee work, a recommendation began to emerge to postpone the celebration of Confirmation to the minimum age of 16 or 17. Since this proposal would mean a period of about three years without Confirmation for young people in most parishes (where the age of the young candidates varied from 10 to 13), the question arose as to what to do during that three year interval. The focus turned to the initiating parish community, and what could be done to enhance its mission and ministry. Even though the minimum age of 16 or 17 was not accepted by Archbishop Gerety, the seeds of an idea for a parish renewal process had been planted in those discussions, and were to bear fruit later in RENEW.

RENEW

At the conclusion of my first year as Archdiocesan Director of Religious Education, I sent a report to Archbishop Gerety. Included in that report was the following reflection:

The next major area to discuss is the preparation of our parish communities for the Adult Catechumenate...I think it can provide a goal for a three-year parish renewal program throughout our Archdiocese to begin in September, 1977, and extend until June, 1980. I hope we could draw together a number of diocesan agencies to serve in providing a unified program of parish renewal for this three-year period. I would see this falling under the aegis of the Office of Pastoral Renewal and would like the Religious Education Center and the Office of Divine Worship to work closely with [Father] Tom Kleissler if such a project were deemed feasible by yourself and your consultors. Other diocesan agencies which could be brought into the process of planning this program could be the School Office, Family Life, Communications, Cursillo, Marriage Encounter, Continuing Education of Priests, the Seminary, the *Advocate* [the Archdiocesan newspaper], and resource people from Justice and Peace. We could design a program, spread out over six semesters, during which parishioners could reflect upon the Mission of their parish in light of the Archdiocesan Mission, and evaluate and revitalize the ministries and the use of the resources within their parish. Rather than have a lot of diversified programs being poured "through a funnel" on top of the head of our pastors (cf. Bishop Ottenweller's remarks at the November Bishops' meeting), we could provide a coordinated and integrated program of renewal which could be integrated into all the current activities of the parish. This could be done within the context of Total Parish Religious Education by developing themes which could be reflected upon during the Sunday Liturgical celebration as well as during the meeting times of various parish societies and programs. We ought to make greater use of video-tape and public television as well as the press and radio in the parish renewal effort. Six themes which might be considered during this three-year period are: 1) Hearing the Word of God and Faith; 2) Personal Relationship with God and Jesus Christ; 3) The Holy Spirit; 4) Conversion; 5) The Church; and 6) The Mission of

Evangelization. This would lead slowly but surely to our three-year goal of preparing a parish to conduct an adult catechumenate by 1980. Much more thought has to be put into such a renewal program, but I would appreciate some reaction from yourself so that if you approve of further investigation, we can initiate a committee this Fall to begin the planning.

When Archbishop Gerety interviewed me about this report, he immediately zeroed in on that section and wanted to get some people together to discuss its viability. Father Tom Kleissler from the Office of Pastoral Renewal and I gathered a plenary session of pastoral leaders from parishes and diocesan staff members, and presented the outline of a three-year spiritual renewal process for parishes. Following the enthusiastic response, there began the demanding work of putting together all the elements. It was an exciting and energizing time for all the diocesan office staff members and parish leaders who collaborated on this project. Spiritual renewal was a theme to which we could all contribute as well as from which we could benefit, and we felt affirmed and encouraged by Archbishop Gerety's support. Our timeline was extended, our topics became more focused, and with the help of Father Cassian Yuhaus, C.P., we tightened some loose ends and structured a training session for parish leadership teams. After piloting RENEW in four different kinds of parishes in the Archdiocese, we began to visit pastoral staffs to invite them to be part of this process. Archbishop Gerety did not want to mandate RENEW, but we were pleased that 200 parishes, 80% of the total in our Archdiocese, agreed to be part of RENEW.

The overall theme presented to the parish leaders at the training sessions during the first season was: Renewed Christian Living in a Renewed Church. Options were made available for Sunday Masses, including homilies and musical suggestions, as well as for small discussion groups, large group activities and home activities. Beginning in the Fall of 1978, the next five seasons focused on the following themes:

The Lord's Call (Fall 1978). We are people in need and the Lord seeks to answer our need (God's loving initiative and our vocation).

Our Response to the Lord's Call (Lent 1979). We turn from our sins and towards the Lord (Conversion Process).

Empowerment by the Spirit (Fall 1979). With the help of the Spirit we try to live justly.

Discipleship (Lent 1980). We undergo conversion as Church for mission to others.

Evangelization (Fall 1980). We reach out to bring the Good News to all.

Three goals permeated this process. RENEW aimed at renewing lives and the life of the Church through learning about the witnessing to the Lord, through formation of people to act with justice, and through the development of vibrant faith communities. We freely acknowledged that true growth cannot come simply from participation in a program; it is the work of the Holy Spirit within hearts which are open that brings about growth and renewal.

In the Archdiocese of Newark, RENEW helped to facilitate some of the liturgical changes which were called for at that time, and it was useful in forming lay leadership, small Christian communities and an appreciation for the Adult Catechumenate. Before RENEW had completed its final season in the Newark Archdiocese, other dioceses in the United States had begun to inquire about its effectiveness. Since 1980, 126 dioceses in the United States have initiated the RENEW process, as well as 98 dioceses in 14 countries around the world, including six dioceses in the Philippines, three in Cameroon, ten in Nigeria, fourteen in South Africa, nine in Australia, fourteen in Canada, seven in Central America, fourteen in India, six in New Zealand, nine in Australia, and four in Scotland.

BAPTISMAL GUIDELINES

The Order of Christian Initiation of Adults was restored as theologically normative by the Second Vatican Council, but the pastoral practice in our Church also continues to celebrate the baptism of infants. The assumption is that the infants will be formed in their faith by their parents and local faith community, and this has become even more necessary in recent years. As Archbishop Gerety wrote in his letter of February 2, 1981, promulgating the Baptismal Guidelines for the Archdiocese of Newark:

The contemporary cultural situation calls for new pastoral methods to prepare people for Christian initiation and sacramental celebration. The revised sacramental rituals are best appreciated when there is proper catechetical preparation and pastoral follow-up. The local parish faith community has a serious responsibility to support and nurture the faith development of those who become baptized, whether adults or infants. This responsibility should be greatly assisted by the annual parish Lenten-Easter program and the services of the Baptismal Ministry Team called for in these guidelines.

The Newark Guidelines sought to respect the two great pastoral principles enunciated in the October 1980 *Instructions on Infant Baptism* issued by the Sacred Congregation for the Doctrine of the Faith. The first states the value of infant baptism, and the second requires some assurance regarding post-baptismal catechesis:

> Assurances must be given that the gift thus granted can grow by an authentic education in the faith and Christian life, in order to fulfill the true meaning of the sacrament. As a rule, these assurances are to be given by the parents or close relatives, although various substitutions are possible within the Christian community. But if these assurances are not really serious there can be grounds for delaying the sacrament; and if they are certainly non-existent the sacrament should even be refused. (paragraph 28)

In the first two paragraphs of the Baptismal Guidelines, the theological norm of adult initiation is stated and the reality of the contemporary pastoral situation is acknowledged:

> 1. The Second Vatican Council called upon the Church to revise its ritual celebrations of entry into the Church in order to express more clearly the process of initiation within the faith community. Of the revised rites, the most significant is the **Rite of Christian Initiation of Adults** (1972) which recommends the framework of the catechumenate. The Christian life is seen as a developing process in which the gift of faith grows to maturity. Based on the biblical doctrine of conversion, the renewed liturgical celebrations of initiation in the Catechumenate stress the adult nature of faith commitment and the explicit intention of the person who knowingly seeks entrance into the Church. Any program of preparation for entrance into the Church should take into account the principles of formation found in the **Rite of Christian Initiation of Adults**. The sacramental guidelines of the Archdiocese of Newark are based on the ecclesiology of the **Rite of Christian Initiation of Adults**. A reflective reading of the Introduction to the R.C.I.A (provided in the Baptism Resource Booklet) will serve as a good background for appreciating the pastoral direction of these Guidelines.

2. In the present pastoral situation, most new members of the Church enter as infants or children. While this practice has been part of the Church's tradition for over a millennium, its preparation and celebration must be adjusted to reflect more clearly that it is analogous to the active faith response which only an adult can give to God's call to conversion. Emphasis is once again being placed on the adult process of becoming a Christian, both for the adult entering into the faith community as well as for the parents and sponsors who speak for the child and who will seek to nurture the same process of conversion in their child. (cf. *Rite of Baptism for Children*, paragraphs 1, 2 and 3.)

Christian initiation takes place within the context of a faith community. The local parish represents the Church for the candidates and serves as their initiating community. The catechumenal process assumes that the parish community is aware of its continuing mission to introduce new members to a living Christian faith and to engage them in the ongoing process of conversion as disciples of Jesus Christ. The Newark Guidelines call for each parish to use the Lenten and Easter Seasons to deepen this awareness of its identity as an initiating community. The Spiritual Life Committee, with the pastoral staff, is responsible for coordinating this annual period of renewal.

Ministering within this broader parish context, the Baptismal Ministry Team is asked to oversee these responsibilities in paragraph 27:

a. Establish a spirit of parish hospitality toward the catechumens, sponsors, and the parents of the infants and children.

b. Place the preparation catechesis within the context of the faith community as a praying, initiating, nurturing, ministering and supporting Church community willing to become involved with the catechumens and families of children as they begin this process of initiation.

c. Integrate the baptism program into the life of the parish as a whole and into the other programs of sacramental preparation.

d. Plan and coordinate a multi-dimensional process of catechesis for the catechumens, sponsors, and parents of the children.

e. Prepare the team's baptismal ministers to serve as catechists, family and hospital ministers.

f. Coordinate where possible the preparation program to the liturgical year.

g. Take into consideration the religious background, evolving family models, and cultural differences among people in their planning process.

h. Be sensitive to the pastoral concerns with regard to the individuals and families within the program.

i. Respond in ministry to the possible crises that develop.

j. Oversee the organizational and administrative aspect of the program, such as record keeping, maintaining a general program file, making known to the parish the members of the baptismal ministry team, etc.

k. Call forth men and women from the parish community who are parents, to serve and be recognized as baptismal ministers for other parents seeking baptism for their children. These parents should be:

    1. Spiritual leaders within the parish community.

    2. Able to relate well with people.

    3. Willing to share their faith with other parents.

    4. Able to devote time for team development and in ministerial outreach.

The Guidelines provide an entire section devoted to the preparation of the family for the baptism of infants and children. Indiscriminate celebrations of baptism are not permitted in the light of the norms given in the revised rites of initiation (paragraph 46 of Guidelines). The timing for the period of preparation is a minimum of two months, allowing for a pastoral visit and a program of catechetical and liturgical preparation. Post-baptismal ministry is also encouraged by means of parish and family ministry programs for parents.

MINISTERIAL DEVELOPMENT CENTER

RENEW and the catechumenal process contributed to the inspiration which led to the establishment of the Newark Archdiocesan Ministerial Development Center. After a year-long assessment of pastoral needs throughout the Archdiocese, Brother Miguel Compos launched the Center at Seton Hall University in October, 1983, with the encouragement and support of Archbishop Gerety. The ecclesial vision of the Archbishop held that discipleship and ministry are inseparable, and that laypeople should be enabled for ministry in the Church and in society. A number of Archdiocesan agencies coordinated their ministerial formation programs with the Ministerial Center, and this led to greater collaboration among the ministries and less duplication of effort. Currently there are fourteen formation Centers throughout the four counties of the Newark Archdiocese, offering courses in both English and Spanish. Candidates are nominated by their pastors to participate in the three year formation process, consisting of three eight-session courses each year. After each course there is a day for retreat and a practicum experience for the candidates. The outline of the courses is as follows:

Year 1   Fall Cycle: The Old Testament and Spirituality: Israel's Journey/Our Journey
Winter Cycle: The Gospel and Spirituality: Christ's Journey/Our Journey
Spring Cycle: The Sacraments: Experiencing God's Presence

Year 2   Fall Cycle: The Church: Journeying in Community
Winter Cycle: Christian Living: Meeting the Moral Demands of Discipleship
Spring Cycle: The Year of the Lord: Living the Paschal Mystery in the Liturgical Cycle

Year 3   Fall Cycle: Spirituality and Ministry: Responding to the Signs of the Times
Winter Cycle: A Ministerial Community: Evangelizing and Becoming Evangelized
Spring Cycle: Corporate Ministry: Sharing Responsibility in the Community

ARCHDIOCESAN PASTORAL DIRECTION

When RENEW was completing its three-year process in the Archdiocese of Newark, there was some confusion among parish leadership with regard to its follow-up. Some wanted to go the route of small Christian communities and others wanted to start the Adult Catechumenate. Archbishop Gerety invited Monsignor Tom Kleissler and me to discuss with him how both of these instruments of renewal could be implemented without conflict. We agreed that it was not a matter of "either...or" but "both...and," and this led to the Archbishop's challenge to "get it together." After considerable consultation and planning, a pastoral direction statement for parishes was developed which we called "Conversion and Community."

This pastoral direction sought to integrate the development of small Christian communities with the pastoral principles of the Adult

Catechumenate. We hoped to meet a twofold concern, while providing a viable structure for the parish of the future. First, we wanted the small communities in the parish to contribute to renewal within the mainstream of Church life and not become elitist or cultist. The pastoral principles derived from the Catechumenate would help to address that concern. Secondly, we wanted to provide adequate support to the candidates journeying through the catechumenal process, and the small Christian communities would provide that support. Several excerpts from the Pastoral Direction statement illustrate this.

The Parish as a Community of Communities

The beautiful simplicity of the small communities approach becomes further apparent by the natural integration it has with our present parish structure. No reorganization of the parish plant is necessary; no heavy expenditure of resources is required. The change relates to the ways we have developed of being Church and ministering to the entire parish community. What is called for is the sharing of a vision, a conviction that where two or three are gathered in his name, God's Spirit is present. Small communities will have a leavening and transforming effect upon family life and the larger parish community. They renew from within and they make parishioners more aware of the Holy Spirit in their midst.

The small groups in turn look to the wider community for support, sacramental life and a sense of belonging. The parish prevents small Christian communities from becoming in-grown and narrow. Like cells in an organism, the small communities make the parish body whole and healthy. Indeed, from its earliest times the Church has been a community of communities.

The Elements of Small Christian Communities

The vital impact of small Christian communities upon the larger parish body will take various shapes and forms. Every small community has an inner dynamic that must eventually reach outward. The awareness of what it means to believe in Jesus Christ will result in new friendships based on a common sharing of values, in a greater appreciation of the Scriptures and a deeper personal relationship with God, in mutual support and affirmation, in a more informed understanding of Catholic faith and principles, and in an outreach in service and evangelization both to the parish community and far beyond. Together we journey with one another to our God.

The Faith Journey as Stages of Christian Initiation and Development

This faith journey that engages all of us is highlighted clearly by the pastoral principles derived from the *Rite of Christian Initiation of Adults*. The restoration of the adult catechumenate was called for by the Second Vatican Council as the means of supporting the conversion process of candidates becoming members of the Catholic Church. The same pastoral principles which characterize this initiation process are likewise valid for the entire parish including small Christian communities.

These principles give promise of a vibrant parish community wherein parishioners:
1. Reach out in the spirit of sharing the good news, inviting all, especially the unchurched, the alienated, and the indifferent to experience God's love.
2. Develop in the midst of the community, by means of Church teachings which offer meaning to their lives, liturgies which celebrate and enhance spiritual growth, and apostolic involvements which are expressions of ever-deepening commitment.
3. Experience opportunities for spiritual renewal, reconciliation, and healing in the process of ongoing conversion.
4. Celebrate the journey of faith by sacramental rituals and other symbolic activities.
5. Seek to affirm each other's gifts and to enable one another to participate actively in the Church's mission through the ministries of Word, Worship, Community Building and Service.

Practical Implementation

This pastoral direction focuses on conversion and community. It speaks to these concepts not merely as separate entities, but even more of a style of parish life that reflects these emphases in all parish activities.

Towards the accomplishment of this goal two leadership communities are encouraged in each parish that would relate to and be closely coordinated by the parish pastoral council.

The first of these leadership communities would center on conversion. The basic responsibility of this community is constantly to invite believers into environments in which they are more able to hear God speaking to them, to experience more deeply God's love, and thus respond more fully to his invitation to growth. This core community would seek to place emphasis on the implementation of the *Rite of Christian*

Initiation of Adults as a viable and effective means of serving those inquiring about our faith as well as a means of integrating spiritual renewal within ongoing parish life.

The second leadership community would be a community for small community development. Its responsibility would be to encourage and aid the implementation of the small community aspect of the archdiocesan pastoral direction in all aspects of parish life. This would include aiding and training leaders of faith sharing communities, helping parish communities take on a more prayerful and communal style, and urging the utilization of small communities as a basis for all ministries and as a means by which parish ministries may better flourish.

In 1993–94 parishes of the Archdiocese of Newark were involved in a year-long process leading to the Archdiocesan Synod held at Seton Hall University, October 7–9. It is interesting to note that the top four recommendations of the synod could be addressed by the Pastoral Direction articulated ten years earlier: Development of Lay Leadership, Lifelong Religious Education/Formation, Building Parish Community and a Caring Church. As the year 2000 is approached, the groundwork laid by Archbishop Gerety continues to serve the Church well.

CONCLUSION

By focusing on spiritual renewal, Archbishop Gerety managed to keep many aspects of Church life in perspective. The Archdiocesan debt of $40 million was paid by 1984, and many of the tensions provoked by the Second Vatican Council were resolved in a pastoral manner. Just as many great leaders have some detractors, so Archbishop Gerety had to contend with some who did not share his enthusiasm for the vision of the Second Vatican Council. Maintaining that one had to "keep chipping away" and that one had to "have the skin of a rhinoceros," Archbishop Gerety persevered in his implementation of the Council until his retirement in 1986. His ecclesial vision and spiritual legacy lives on in the hearts of many faithful members of our Church, both within and far beyond the borders of the Archdiocese of Newark.

8

Education: Keystone to Success

Marguerite O'Connor

Parish life in Blessed Martin de Porres Church in New Haven, Connecticut, in 1953 showed great promise when Father Peter L. Gerety, the Pastor, sought permission from Archbishop Henry J. O'Brien to open the first interracial parochial school in the Archdiocese of Hartford. The growth of his Parish was such that concern for the spiritual and educational needs of the youth was of prime importance to him. At the recommendation of his brother priests he contacted the Provincial Superior of the Sisters of Notre Dame, Sister Loretta Julie, in Waltham, Massachusetts, who, after an interview, agreed to provide two Sisters.

At a later time the Sister Provincial shared with her Sisters the fact she had intended to refuse Father due to the numberless requests being made on the Province at that time for Sisters. When Father noticed her hesitancy he told her he had read the life of the Foundress, Blessed Julie Billiart who had shared with her Sisters years ago that the Congregation was founded to meet the educational needs of children in the most needy locations. She was taken by surprise at what he had learned about the Congregation and stated afterward that it was impossible for her to give a negative answer.

The two Sister teachers chosen were Sister Leo Margaret and Sister Elizabeth St. James who would be living with their own Religious Sisterhood at St. Boniface Convent in New Haven until their convent would be built.

The old St. Mary's School on Ashmun Street, which had been vacated for some years by the Dominican Sisters, was to become Blessed Martin de Porres School.

On August 10, 1954 both Sister Leo Margaret and Sister Elizabeth

St. James arrived at St. Boniface Convent and were warmly welcomed by their own Sisters as well as by Father Gerety who phoned and made arrangements to have them meet with the parishioners at the Children's Mass the following day.

It was necessary to see the streets where the Projects of thirteen-story high buildings lined the horizon on the way to Church. It was an awesome picture. However, on arrival at Blessed Martin de Porres Church the welcome carpet was out as Father Leo Gerety and Father Patrick Speer, his Associate, greeted the Sisters who were surrounded by little ones trying to get a peek. Time was taken to introduce each child. This gesture made a significant impact on the Sisters as to just how special each child was. The Liturgy was most impressive and joy charged the atmosphere. Also, the parishioners met outside after Mass to speak to both priests and were introduced to the two Sisters.

The following day the Sisters were brought to the old St. Mary's School which was now to be Blessed Martin de Porres School. The newly painted classrooms, shining windows and waxed floors indicated how important it was to provide the best for these little ones. Joy seemed to charge the atmosphere as the Sisters were introduced to their new surroundings.

There had been an earlier registration in June and at the second registration the Sisters met a larger number of little ones and mothers. Anticipation seemed to light the eyes of both children and mothers. Father Speer with Father Gerety performed the introductions and their joyous attitude did much to create an atmosphere of friendliness and understanding with mothers and children. Father Gerety as well as Father Speer was able to give the teachers insights into the home conditions of the children which proved of great help in understanding the children.

Later in exchanging views with one another the Sisters had to admit they were never acquainted with any Pastor or Associate who knew each child by name as well as the name of the parents. This was quite different and proved to be most helpful.

Daily the education of the Sisters increased and so did the registration of the pupils. Mothers particularly wished to talk to the Sisters after class hours. Enrollment increased somewhat the first year but could never compare with the number increase of the ensuing years.

Days flew into weeks and months but not without addressing the religious educational needs of public school students, especially those preparing for the Sacraments of Baptism, Penance, Holy Eucharist and Confirmation.

Parents of the public school children showed much interest in trying to get their children in the school as each year one more grade was to be opened. This was an encouraging sign. As a result of the total summation of the influence of the school, the Church, and the new environment, one must say that the home life changed, showing a great dedication to the school which taught the importance of the family, the togetherness of the family and the responsibility each one has in building all three. It was interesting to see their love for the school and the pride they took to share it with playmates of their Elm Haven Projects. One could see the development of friendships within the school as well as in home environment. They began to cheer one another in class when the right answer emerged. They became the pride of the Projects when uniforms were introduced. We found the children loved them as a signified ownership to them—to their school, their classroom, their teacher, their classmates. Very often they returned in the afternoon after classes because they wanted ownership to include the teachers, the Sisters.

The Family Life Program was initiated so that parents could become more alerted to the spiritual, educational and sociological aspects of developmental stages of their little ones. This was a program which brought mostly mothers to the school weekly. This became a reliable source of faith and has continued to be so. Togetherness was the theme of the group and faith the common denominator. It drew the mothers together in an endeavor to enliven the faith that was deepening with the days. They often met among themselves to share the good and the bad as their family life took a different shape.

Days flew into weeks and months but not without addressing the needs of teenage girls who were invited to join the Sodality of Our Lady. Weekly meetings were well attended, but as the area meetings were scheduled the Sisters wanted St. Martin's girls to favorably measure up to what the Sodality anticipated. However, their faith grew as they came in contact with teenagers of other schools. They could see their own life develop into a love of their faith. It was a group that had daily prayers to say, and when they met they shared the difficulties as well as the enlightenment they gained through spiritual reading. Father Gerety expressed his pride in their desire to be the best of whatever they were and it made a big difference. There seemed to be no difficulty in expressing their sincere views in becoming the best of whoever they were. Devotion to Our Lady has persisted through the years.

Religious education of the public school children from grades two to eight was scheduled for a weekday after school. This worked out quite well as the Winchester School from which most of the children came was just a block down the street. They were eager to learn about God and their Catholic Religion and also eager to be part of the School enrollment.

Father Gerety was always alert to the numberless changes in his parish and always seeking to provide the best for the Church and School which each year seemed to make a deeper impact on home and environment. He was consistently alerted to the innovative programs which Mayor Lee was launching in order to come to terms with issues that were affecting most residents in the Elm Haven District where Blessed Martin's was located. He was successful in receiving one of the largest grants. New Haven launched a war on poverty about four years before the Federal Government's similar efforts began. It was one of the first big money grants to St. Martin's and it affected parents, priests and Sisters in providing yet more for the children.

The beginning of the availability of funding for educational programs coincided with the growth of Blessed Martin's parish school in 1962. It now was having a number of dreams realized, i.e. Pre-Kindergarten, tutorial after school program, team teaching, experimental curriculum and job experience in the schools through a New Haven Foundation Grant of $5,000.

The beginning of the availability of funding coincided with the growth of Blessed Martin's parish school. The first class to compete eight years graduated in June of 1963. The Family Enrichment Program was launched the same year and grew to tremendous proportions in a well-structured curriculum. This was considered the best approach to the spiritual, sociological and psychological aspects of growth in home life. Considering the last sentence I quote from a section of the annals of St. Martin's School:

> Constantly we receive words of commendation, congratulations and encouragement. This does mean much to the work, and we do admit that we see growth, but in each grade the classroom teacher realizes that she must become skilled in the techniques of guidance and trust in the Lord in coping with the emotional problems which can and do disrupt daily lessons.

Adequate guidance facilities can never be given a school subjected to environmental factors such as ours, but the constant efforts to cope with children who are hurting and disturbed can be a great challenge as we gain their trust and relieve their frustrations.

September of 1964 brought tremendous news. Our Reverend Pastor received word he was to be made a Monsignor. The hearts of the priests, Sisters, children and parishioners were gladdened. How eagerly they all looked forward to the Investiture Ceremonies which took place in St. Joseph's Cathedral, Hartford, on October 24 at eight o'clock. It was well represented by Blessed Martin's parishioners.

In October there was much excitement when word was received that the Ford Foundation was awarding Blessed Martin's School a grant of $48,000. Dreams could now be realized for a full-time Librarian and Social Worker. The almost depleted shelves in the Vocational Library also could be enriched.

The Family Enrichment Program which was five months in the offing had grown to tremendous proportions. It was a well-structured program. This was a productive way to get into the homes of the children as every other Wednesday evening the parents assembled in the school for sessions in child psychology with the springboard into religious and home life. This aided the parents to be articulate as they participated in the discussion groups that concluded the evening agenda. "The local councils delighted in relating how well the parents articulated as they participated in the discussion groups that concluded the agenda of the evening. They had learned how to verbalize in the small units provided by the school." Both Monsignor Gerety and Father Speer were pleased when they heard that report. Community had become more meaningful to them now and the importance of family life had taken on a new look. One woman reported at a meeting that her husband told her that she should have attended the sessions earlier because she now was renewing the attitudes reflected in their early years together.

It was recorded that during the summer of 1963 seventeen Yale students and six Albertus Magnus students operated on a forty-hour week basis during the summer months to improve the academic level of achievement for the children. This group had anticipated a summer in Mexico, but on hearing their buddies who were tutors during the year tell of Blessed Martin's youngsters, they decided to be part of the group.

Six Sisters also volunteered to operate in supervisory roles during the summer.

The influence of the Yale boys on the eighth grade students was great. These students would take them to historic places and ball games as well as to lunch and dinners some weekends and shared experiences these youngsters could never experience otherwise. The Albertus Magnus girls also provided similar experiences as well as showing a keen interest in the nursery school tots.

Truly there was no fact that these college students did not share with them. They fostered in them the desire to study and achieve. They endeavored to fulfill what the Guidance Program was designed to achieve in thinking about the future as they applied their attention to their studies.

It also has been recorded at this time in 1963 that Monsignor Gerety had initiated a "FIRST" in coordinating a steering committee on Race Relations among Religious.

The year 1966 brought much joy as well as sadness to the Sisters and parishioners. The greatest event of all was the elevation of Monsignor Gerety to the Episcopacy. Monsignor first broke the news to the Sisters at the Convent Mass on March 8th. They had mixed feelings of being proud and happy that his giftedness was acknowledged, but deeply saddened at the great loss to St. Martin's Parish and to them. At the Sunday Masses the reaction was the same and many came to the Sisters for comfort. The only solace was in the realization that the work of the Lord would be extended far beyond their horizons. The children expressed their joy that their Pastor was to become a Bishop. One youngster spoke privately outside to Monsignor and said, "Father, they make you a Bishop and if you keep on being good they will make you a 'good Sister of Notre Dame.'" The laugh could be heard in all classrooms on the first floor. When Monsignor shared this with the staff it did much to lessen their feelings of loss.

A series of dinners, receptions, etc. followed until the day of his Consecration, June 1st. St. Joseph's Cathedral in Hartford was the setting for the ceremony.

The new Bishop did not leave St. Martin's Parish for Maine until he once more blessed his children by confirming the candidates of the Confirmation class on June 4th, and on June 19th he delivered the address to the Graduates.

The truth is he never will leave the heart of the Blacks in St. Martin's alone because he is revered by all the old and young adults who learned the Gospel message through his caring love and the Blacks will always be at the core of gratitude and love for Archbishop Gerety.

The Blacks will never let their appreciation and love rest alone in the memory of what he has done. It lives in their memory of mind and heart!

Here is an amazing rundown of an amazing person. He was one who saw an answer to a question that was frustrating and he faced it with trust in God. How to help men, women and children find their way in a world of confusion? How? Through education. And he pursued it until he was satisfied that trust in God and education is the way to success.

9

The Option for the Poor

Cassian J. Yuhaus, C.P.

Long before the phrase "option for the poor" became a by-word in the social doctrine of the Church, before people heard of Medellin and Puebla, Archbishop Gerety was in New Haven, CT walking the street with the poor, bringing them food, caring for their sick and above all being a true priest for them, a good pastor, a shepherd. He willingly and lovingly dedicated the major portion of his priesthood to these defenseless and marginalized people of God. And although called to high responsibility in the Church he never abandoned or forgot God's poor. He heard their cry. He felt their plight. And from whatever position of prestige or influence that came to be his, he defended these special people, the Anawim, and became their advocate. I have been privileged to work with and for Archbishop Gerety in those exciting and challenging years of renewal. It is a distinct honor to dedicate this reflection to him in gratitude for the wisdom and courage he shared with me.

1.

Certainly among the more momentous decisions made by the Church in the last 500 years we must place the daring decision made by a man of unusual courage in the face of violent opposition. One hundred years ago Leo XIII, following the inspiration and great example of Emmanuel Wilhelm Von Ketteler, Archbishop of Mainz, turned the face of the Church away from a controlling grip of the powerful landed aristocracy and an arrogant nobility toward the working poor and powerless. It was courageous in the extreme.

The Church, but twenty years before (1871), had lost its lands, its armies, its political power and invested wealth in the bloody revolt of the Italian States against the Papacy, as Cavour from the north and Garibaldi from the south put the irremovable pincers on the famed Papal States. Now this daring Pontiff imprisoned inside the walls of a tiny Vatican garden dared to risk what support he had from the remaining, dominant heads of States and manipulators of financial destinies by his straightforward address to the "utter misery of the masses."

Leo XIII declared: "The momentous gravity of the current state of affairs fills every mind with painful apprehension." He readily admitted, "The discussion is not easy, nor is it void of danger. It is no easy matter to define the relative rights and mutual duties of the rich and the poor."[1]

For one hundred years the Church has struggled to defend those "relative" rights and to clarify those "mutual" duties. But that defense and those clarifications somehow always came from the side of the rich. The subject was the rich. The poor were object, or more correctly, abject.

It was not until our day and the raising-up of yet another prophet, more courageous still, that the Church made an even far more momentous decision: The Church declared its place by preference and destiny to be on the side of the poor. The option for the poor in the life and teachings of Pope John XXIII and in his council may well be the greatest event of our times. The poor become the subject, the rich the object. The renewed Catholic social doctrine begins and proceeds from the side of the poor. We have yet to grasp the significance and consequence of this focus.

Three dangers prevent us from grasping the significance of this momentous change. These three dangers are found both in the Church at large as well as within dioceses, parishes and religious communities, especially of men. These three dangers are: indifference, confusion and escape.

The first and perhaps greatest danger is indifference which leads to apathy. This is seen in the light-handed treatment the profound and revolutionary statements of Catholic social doctrine receive at the hands of many Churchmen. If they were uneducated their stupidity could be excusable. Inexcusable are attitudes contained in expressions such as, "We've heard it all before" or "Here we go again: The poor, the poor— there are so many other items on the agenda" and "Let's get on with it."

The second danger is confusion, confusion about the very premises of social doctrine. Was Jesus political? What right has the Church to interfere in the world of business? Are we not to keep the temporal and the spiritual orders distinct and separate? Should not the Church be concerned about souls and their salvation? This argument is raised to its highest level of obfuscation when we call God to arbitrate: Do we trust in Providence? Is not sacred Scripture enough? The confusion is multiple: Scriptural, Theological and Social.

The third danger is the best cover-up of all: Who are the poor? We are all poor! And, can we not say that the poorest of the poor, without doubt, are the spiritually poor: all those nice people with their furs and their Porsches who mean so well. Furthermore, what about the most difficult of all in the affluent society—the bewildered middle class people. Someone must care for them. And after all "the poor you always have with you" to quote an eminent Rabbi. There are so many, many concerns. The great escape.

The utter vacuity of these three approaches is self evident. The truth is—there *is* no other business on today's agenda. The preferential option for the poor *is* the agenda. Let's get on with that. To do so we need a new look.

There are at least five ways in which the preferential option for the poor should strike us as new and bold, daring and prophetic. We need to catch its freshness, its vigor, its challenge.

1. First, the option is *new* in the way it emerged in our day. It was as unexpected and as unseemly as its precursor, the peasants' pope, John XXIII. It shook the Council profoundly and reversed its trend. But we should have known this from Pope John's opening words to the Council, "The Church is and desires to be the Church of all but principally the Church of the Poor."[2] We must join that statement with the startling remark of Cardinal Lercaro at the close of the first session (December 7, 1962), "The central theme of this Council should be the Church of the poor."

2. Second, it is new in its approach. The option dramatically reverses the traditional approach to the problems of poverty, want and destitution. The traditional approach was always from the side of the rich. It was an approach of compassion, of giving alms, reaching out and caring for the Lazarus at our door. All of it wonderful and good. Somehow we felt we could reverse it all if only the rich would be converted.

That approach utterly failed. There is a limit to the number of band-aids you can put on a wound. The problems of poverty, want and misery must be seen not only from the side of the poor but also with the eyes of the poor. Only this will lead to pro-active not re-active concern.

3. Third, the option for the poor is new in its extent. We are no longer talking about the poor man, the poor woman, the child. We are

talking about classes of poor, entire peoples and populations, races and social groups. We are not talking about "pockets of poverty," we are talking about systemic oppression, unjust laws, oppressive policies, outright criminal discrimination and social degradation. We are focusing on social sin, the sins of a nation, the sins of a Church, the sins of international conglomerates. We are talking about structures of sin. Furthermore, our vision cannot be limited to the local scene. It must be global. We see these as interconnected. We cannot attend to one without the other.

4. Fourth, the option is new in its demands. The task facing all of us is prophetic and imperative. The situation in which we live and to which we contribute is immoral. No one can remain indifferent and claim Christ as Lord. Our tasks are no less than the transformation of the world: calling forth a new humanity, a new way of thinking, acting, sharing in life on this planet: the Christ-revolution.

5. Fifth, the option for the poor is new in its urgency. We cannot continue to live in a society where, as Pope John Paul II has repeatedly warned us, "the rich become richer at the expense of the poor who day by day become poorer."[3] Clearly we are on a collision course. We rightly wonder with Marcel Proust about the glass wall and the dark men: "Whether the glass wall will everlastingly protect the celebrations of the wonderful animals within and whether the dark men who look on avidly in the night will not seize them from their aquarium and devour them."[4] Just a few years ago the Holy See ended its appeal to address the question of international debt with these words, "May our appeal be heeded before it is too late!"[5]

In his final word to us before his death, one of the greatest theologians of our day, Karl Rahner, reflecting on faith in the "wintry season" declared, "...if Christianity really possessed that degree of radical consistency which by nature it demands, then it would be a springtime in the Church....Each one of us should (instead) see these times as a personal challenge to work so that the inner core of faith becomes alive. Then, of course the Church itself will shine radiantly again and it will again become clear that the Church is what it was intended to be, a Sacramental sign of the world's salvation."[6] My dear friend, Archbishop Gerety, was first to call my attention to these prophetic words of a Church luminary he admired so much.

2.

I wish to make a rather simple, declarative statement as the basis for any further discussion about the poor. Surely I will not avoid a direct response to the question that seems to irritate everyone once discussion turns on the option for the poor, namely, "Who are the poor?" But before attempting an answer to that question, let it be said that whatever further truths may be explored, whatever attitudes are shaped or re-shaped in the dialogue, whatever action we shall engage in or disengage from will depend upon our perception and acceptance of a truth at once fresh and bold, stark and alarming before which there is no hiding:

For the contemporary Church as well as for the world of our day the central issue is the poor.

Our success or failure as Church depends upon our perception and our response to this issue. More startling still our success or failure as human beings upon this planet depends upon our perception and response to the poor. We need not play games about survival. This is THE survival issue. Church and Church leaders, States and Statesmen all are divided by the stand they take toward the poor.

Let us now address the question, "Who are the poor?" We may escape the issue by the abstract philosophical answer which is very true, "We are all poor." We could hide the issue in the equally true theological statement "The rich themselves are most frequently the poorest of all." No. That will not do. A direct, straightforward response must be unequivocal.

"Who are the poor?" By the poor we mean the real not the analogous poor. The actual not the theoretical or symbolic poor.

By the poor, we mean indigent and suffering humanity. We mean the economically needy. We mean all who are deprived of the material goods necessary to live with dignity and hope. Above all we mean all those classes of people who are the victims of injustice in whatever form. The exploited, the oppressed, the marginalized. This includes not only the wretched: the beggars, outcasts, abandoned children, but also the exploited workers, the handicapped, physical or mental, as well as the minorities, in particular, the blacks, the aboriginals. In a special way we mean women victimized by unjust, unequal economic, political and social standards.

3.

From Leo XIII through John XXIII to Pope John Paul II: so much has changed in one hundred years. Our approach, our understanding and our response to the poor have all been radicalized. This radical difference is in both directions: The way we look upon the poor and the way the poor look upon us. In this look we discover our response.

In times past it was the individual poor person about whom we were concerned. We "treated" the poor case. We "looked after" the poor family across the tracks. We prayed for the poor man. Not that we shall ever cease to be concerned about a particular poor person. Today the entire context has changed. We will never resolve the problems of destitute poverty case by case. Today we must look upon entire classes of poor: masses of destitute and marginalized peoples. Entire groups. Whole nations.

And that leads us directly to a second radical approach. The poor are not poor because they want to be poor, despite the absurd reference of a recent president of the United States. They are not poor because they are lazy and obnoxious by the standards of the wealthy and well-to-do. They are poor because they are *made* poor and they are poor because they are *kept* poor. The masses of poor people are victims of unjust laws and unjust systems. And these laws and systems lock them out of the mainstreams of human life and development and lock them into their prisons of wretchedness while some of us pass by, look in and feel sad, for a few moments at least. We say to one another, "It's too bad."

Well, it is too bad. It is too bad for the rest of us. We may not be so indifferent and casual without grave danger to ourselves and to our children's children.

Lazarus, of old, did sit alone at the gate. Lazarus, of old, did beg for a crumb. He trusted in God and hoped for a better world after a mean life in this. Some few of us were moved to pity. But today Lazarus is not alone. There are simply too many of them. And they are no longer whimpering for a pittance. They are rising up. They, too, read the Gospel, the Gospel of justice and human rights. They, too, read the papers. They see the commercials. They feel the inequity and they demand justice. While we seem powerless to change the situation, they are becoming empowered to take things into their own hands. Joined with countless others on both sides of the track, they strive for a better life for all, here and hereafter. And they shall overcome.

There is yet another way of getting a handle on all this. In their inciteful and challenging study, to which I am deeply indebted, Pixley and Boff, eminent scholars and theologians, urge us to approach the almost incomprehensible situation of massive poverty and destitution by seeing the poor in three categories.[7]

Of category one, we are all very well aware. Medellin and Puebla gave us the new terminology to better understand their plight. In the first category are the "marginalized," "the exploited poor"—all those who are forced to live outside the prevailing economic system or who are excluded from participation in it.

Marginalized are the outcasts: the abandoned children; the unemployed; the starving lost people; beggars; the wretched. "Exploited" are so many migrant workers, tenant farmers, immigrants, service people of all kinds who must accept part-time work with no benefits whatsoever. Of these, too, we are all aware.

There is a second very large category of poor. We experience them daily but of these we do not want to be aware. These poor are victims of unhealthy attitudes, unjust practices and policies; victims of our discriminatory laws and customs; victims of discrimination by reason of race or creed or sex or ethnic origin. Our aboriginal people belong here, our deprived Afro-Americans belong here, and above all women belong here.

There is a third category of poor where the radicalization of this new approach, our renewed understanding and our response to the poor is immediately evident. Unlike times past, in our day a new class of poor has arisen. They make clear to us that the poor are not only the people "out there," in other lands or in the ghettos and slums of our urban centers. They are everywhere: in our homes, in our overcrowded prisons, in our hospitals, in our streets: the drug-addicts, the handicapped, physically or mentally, the suicidally depressed, the homeless, the aged, the unemployable. And these "new poor" are spewed-up everyday as the social economic system proves itself increasingly inept and unable to respond to the injustice. Without radical transformation from within we shall never be able to respond.

4.

The closer one gets to the problem of the poor in our day, the more overwhelming does it become. There is the danger all too prevalent among us of giving up all hope of changing the situation. "What can *I* do?" "Would that there were some way I could help. But what can one person do?"

As this attitude prevails, the complexity increases. There is much we can and we must do. Permit me to offer a few suggestions about where we might begin and how we may proceed.

I propose we begin with two truths with which every effort to address the issue of the poor should begin. They are foundational, intrinsic and indispensable.

In a way the common complaint referred to above, about what one person can do, is quite right. Individually and alone, there is not much that we can do in any area of life. But the attitude itself is mistaken. It fails to recognize the most important truth about ourselves: we were never intended to live alone. We cannot exist alone. By our very nature we are social, dialogical and relational. Our life is fulfilled only in, with and through one another. The dominant American individualism is not only erroneous, it is extremely dangerous. Not only does it make us unable to address the most urgent problems of our time but it erodes the very foundations of our society.[8]

Our mutual interdependence (permit the redundance) is not just a matter of family structure. We are interdependent socially, politically and economically. This interdependent nature is the foundation for the realization of our own worth, our personal dignity. It is the assurance of our freedoms. By God's design we are essentially social. We are necessarily and irrevocably interconnected. We belong together. We have power over one another.

For the first time in human history, science and technology have enabled us to relearn in unforgettable ways the basic oneness and unity of the human family. What we are relearning is that essentially we are undifferentiated. Increasingly we are commingled. Critically, we are interdependent. This may well be the most significant explosion of our day.

Solidarity is the reality of human existence and its first hope for survival. We are tightly bound together across and around this small village-home which no one of us owns, all of us receive co-equally, each calls home and all must share justly. We are all on-line. This is the first and the basic truth with which to begin our valiant effort to resolve the grave situation which the Church sums up as "the preferential option for the poor."

The second truth upon which we base every effort to understand and to respond to the problem of the poor is a matter of Gospel teaching.

More, it is the substance of Gospel morality. The distinguishing mark of the disciple of Jesus, his/her foremost characteristic, is a deep love for others expressed in a willing and preferential response to the need of the other in the concrete experiences of life. The follower of Jesus, obedient to the Gospel, becomes a "Whatsoever person." When all is said and done in my life, only one thing matters, "Whatsoever you did to the least of these my brethren, you did unto Me."⁹ Christian love, Christian justice, human righters and human dignity are the "seamless garment." They are all of a *piece* and are the basis of peace and happiness here and hereafter.

The recognition of these two basic truths: the interdependence of the human family and the primacy of love in Christian life, lead us directly to the affirmation of further illuminating principles. These are contained in the truths just enunciated and flow from them.

The first is the priority we assign to spiritual values over material ones. While beautifully and inseparably united in the oneness of the human person, spiritual needs, spiritual values are distinguishable from physical needs and physical values. The primacy belongs to the spiritual: love, freedom, justice, truth. These endow the physical with meaning and value; they control, direct and enable the physical. My physical needs, your physical needs, the physical needs of all of us can be met only when and only if the spiritual needs of each are respected and sustained.

The second principle follows: Created by God, created for God in the very image and likeness of God, each person is eternally sacred: of whatever color, creed, race or sex. Each is endowed from the moment of conception in this world to the moment of inception into the next with a certain inalienable dignity, with human rights that are to be sustained at every stage of life. This single unchangeable regard within a wide spectrum of different expressions makes each of us sacred: the unborn, the babies, children, youth, the middle aged, the old and infirm.

The third principle addresses the context of this entire reflection. Not only are we essentially interdependent as humans, we are also interdependent as village dwellers with all the other animals and with the living earth itself. The integrity of creation means precisely that we live together within the earth system in a respectful and harmonious relationship whereby all life is held sacred and the life-giving systems upon which we all depend for happiness, growth and development are safeguarded and guaranteed for all.

5.

In addressing the foundational truths and principles for the Christian response to the poor, the Church appeals not only to the highest truths of divine revelation but to the highest and noblest instincts of the human heart. It all sounds very utopian, overly optimistic. Not so. The Church and Churchmen and women have been around too long to fall into the trap of idle dreaming. We acknowledge the fearful reality. We are on a collision course. Our world is divided between the few and the many; between the haves and the have nots; between the privileged and the deprived; between the rich who daily become richer at the expense of the poor who daily become poorer; between the powerful and the powerless.

The super-struggle today is not between super-powers. It is between two great socio-cultural systems in severe tension and in dread of each other:

- the super-culture of high technology and sophisticated science and
- the much larger and more traditional culture of the poor throughout the world.

Neither can exist without the other. A threat to one is a threat to the other. Little success has been made in working out a suitable equation for the well-being of both. The issue is whether we shall form a renewed vision of life as sacred and noble for all, as possible and achievable for all, or whether we shall continue to widen the gap between us.

We shall not attain this vision unless, as Pope John Paul II so poignantly reminds us, we name the devils that afflict us, unless we identify the root of the evils that threaten to destroy us. These are seen to be two: "The all consuming desire for profit and...the thirst for power with the intent of imposing one's will upon others." He further states: "not only do individuals fall victim to this double attitude of sin, nations and blocs can do so too...it is a question of moral evil, the fruit of many sins which lead to structures of sin."[10]

This, then, is really the heart of the matter. Our situation today is entirely different. Our challenge is to change the structures that maintain systems of injustice, exploitation and inequity. Our challenge is to utilize the amazing new powers of resource and discovery to find a valid and creative response for the transformation of society, the reshaping of our world. Our challenge is to overcome apathy and indifference, fear and ignorance and dare to create from among examined alternatives a better world for all peoples, rich and poor alike.

In embracing and proclaiming a preferential option for the poor, the Church and Church people oblige themselves to repudiate any alliance, political or social, with those who unjustly hold power or privilege in society. It means, as Pope John Paul declares explicitly, "to be in solidarity" with all categories of people so as to effect structural change that alone will eliminate systems of injustice.[11]

The Church courageously accepts the challenge for herself in the first place. "*Anyone* who ventures to speak to people about justice must first *be just* in their eyes. We must undertake an examination of the modes of acting, and of the possessions and life-style found within the Church itself."[12] Many of us feel it is time that just such an examination be made in earnest.

All of us who accept discipleship with Jesus must take our stand as he did on the side of the poor. "Today more than ever the Word of God will be unable to be proclaimed and heard unless it is *accompanied by the witness* of the power of the Holy Spirit, working within the actions of Christians in the service of their brothers."[13]

"In the service of their brothers." Archbishop Gerety wanted and desired nothing more than to serve his brothers, his brother Bishops, his brother Priests, his sister and brother religious, and above all the people of God, especially the poor.

Endnotes

1. *Rerum Novarum*, May 15, 1891, 1–3.

2. Pope John XXIII, Address announcing the opening of Vatican Council II, September 7, 1962.

3. John Paul II, *Sollicitudo Rei Socialis*, December 30, 1987, art. 14.

4. Marcel Proust, as quoted in *The Bible, the Church and the Poor*, by J. Pixley and C. Boff, (London: Burns and Oates, 1989).

5. John Paul II, "At the Service of the Human Community: An Ethical Approach to the International Debt Question," December 27, 1986.

6. Karl Rahner, *Faith in a Wintry Season* (Crossroad, 1990).

7. *The Bible, the Church and the Poor*, op. cit.

8. Robert N. Bellah et al., *Habits of the Heart* (University of California Press, 1985).

9. Mt 26:31–46.

10. John Paul II, *Sollicitudo Rei Socialis*, par 37.

11. Ibid., par. 40.

12. *Justitia in Mundo*, Synodal document, 1971, par. 46.

13. Paul VI, *Octogesima Adveniens*, 1971, par. 51.

10

Universe Reveals God's Secrets

Mary C. McGuinness, O.P.

For you there is only one road that can lead to God and this is fidelity to remain constantly true to yourself, to what you feel is highest in you. The road will open before you as you go. (Teilhard de Chardin)

In order to remain true to myself and faithful to the call which God has graciously gifted me, I want to share with you, Archbishop Gerety, some thoughts about the new story of the universe. It is a story that is quickly unfolding because of recent scientific discoveries about the origin and development of this vast universe. It is often referred to as a "new cosmology." As Archbishop of Newark, you were always so open to creative ideas when I worked with you as staff person to the Archdiocesan Pastoral Council (1979 to 1985). Your energetic and resourceful leadership brought alive the spirit of Vatican II.

So I dedicate this essay to you and invite you, Archbishop Gerety, to enter into the contemplation and study of this new story and urge you to promote dialogue and disputation around it wherever you can as best you can. Because you are such a lover of sailing, I am sure that the lure of nature has captivated your heart and brought you to a deeper realization of the creative Spirit who has brought forth this magnificent universe. May you seize this new moment of grace.

For a number of years I have been reading, studying, praying about the new cosmology. Thomas Berry, Brian Swimme, Miriam Therese MacGillis, my friend and Dominican sister, and many others have influenced and taught me the evolving story of our universe and our beautiful planet Earth. Also as a member of the Dominican Sisters of Caldwell, I have been associated for twelve years with Genesis Farm, Blairstown, New Jersey, a learning center for earth literacy. Genesis

Farm has been a wonderful gift to our community and a meaningful ministry to the thousands who have come to learn more about Earth and how to live and appreciate the interrelationships of its being.

Happily our entire congregation and my local community at Our Lady of the Lake in Verona, NJ have also begun to study and to dialogue, and enter into disputation (in the true Dominican way) about the new story, as it is simply called. Our community chapter set three directions for the future: 1) to reclaim our passion for contemplation, 2) to promote justice in every area of our congregation, and 3) to deepen our study, living and teaching of the mysteries of the universe and the sacredness of all creation and to resist the ongoing devastation of our planet.

It has taken our congregation as a whole a long time to come to this moment of grace. I question why. I question why, too, it has taken the churches so long. While millions of individual people, groups and some communities have taken notice of the ruinous assault on planet Earth, Berry claims that "the religious traditions of America have taken no serious notice of what is happening, nor have they offered leadership in remedying a situation which is as devastating in its spiritual as it is in its physical aspects." While other groups and organizations are committed to arresting or reversing this devastation, Berry believes they "cannot succeed without assistance from our religious traditions." I offer here some reflections on the revolutionary universe story. For me it means that I am here today because of an evolutionary process that God set in motion billions of years ago through which everything continues to evolve today. I am only one small person in that process, one creature among many living creatures. We have only recently discovered that our solar system came into existence through the collapse of a former star in the Milky Way Galaxy. Similarly, we have recently realized that our small planet Earth is the only offspring of that star. Earth has continued to evolve, becoming a living, blue green organism, alive, changing and expressing itself through all the different varieties of plants, insects, animals, fish, birds, and humans, which have come to be.

This evolutionary process allowed so many wonderful species to develop, all interrelated, all interdependent; all called to respect and reverence each other, to work together to make sure each living creature is regarded as kin.

In the Judeo-Christian tradition, the creation stories of Genesis 1 and 2 revealed that we were asked to name the animals and plants and to have dominion over them and subdue Earth. These stories supported a belief that humans were superior beings who could take from our Earth whatever we wanted to benefit ourselves, to prosper and develop. We felt we could use "resources" of our planet to "improve our way of life" regardless of the injury we might wreak upon our Earth home.

And we did! We mined the minerals of Earth, turned herds into endangered species, stripped forests and paved farmland. We did many things "to develop" what we thought was a better way of life. In so doing we raced through the industrial revolution, the scientific age, the technological age and down the information superhighway. All brought humankind many benefits but in the process we raped Earth, polluted her waters, and destroyed very precious eco-systems. We often did this in a very thoughtless way because we considered Earth "just a thing," "simply matter," a backdrop for our human destiny.

Yet a dual transformation has taken place because of that very license to subdue nature. For example, as technology developed, we could explore with a microscope the tiniest particles of life and then a whole new mystical world opened up for us. We saw worlds inside tiny cells, molecules, atoms and, lo and behold, we discovered that in each atom, protons and neutrons and electrons were not stationary but in motion. They indeed had a life of their own, interacting with each other, and within them were other tinier particles all held in webs of relationships and order, which our language could not explain.

We have come to observe that the interior of atoms reveals a basic signature of God in their very structure. Four mysterious inner forces are found in each and every nucleus: an electromagnetic force, a gravitational force, a strong nuclear force, and a weak nuclear force. No atom exists that does not adhere to these forces. All atoms comprising the total universe are bound by these forces which reveal the absolute unity of all that exists. The universe is one. What Jesus prayed that we might come to realize is, in fact, now observable.

Looking at outer space, scientists explored planets and galaxies and discovered new stars being born and whole new galaxies appearing beyond our Milky Way Galaxy. The universe was alive, is alive, and is constantly expanding.

With scientific worlds unfolding, humans came to a new consciousness: that we, as part of this evolutionary process, are, indeed, the universe, and, more precisely, Earth emerging into self-consciousness. This realization finally put our human community into a position where we can rethink who we really are and what our relationship to planet

Earth and to the universe really means. It invites us to go back to the Genesis accounts of scripture and to interpret them in the altered light of recent discoveries. It invites us to come home to Earth and realize we and Earth are one.

One of the ideas that we learn in Genesis is that we are made in the image and likeness of God. As I reflect upon the words "being made in the image of God" I believe, among other things, it means we are made to be relational. Our Christian tradition teaches that our God is relational—a triune God, a trinity of Persons, each in relation to the other and each in relationship to all of creation.

"Made in the image of God" and "relational" mean we are companions on Earth, companions with God, with other human beings, with all of creation. We are one of many magnificent creations, one to be in companionship with the birds, animals, sea creatures, all trees, herbs, vegetables, flowering plants, etc. We are called to complement and interact with one another so all can live in harmony and peaceful accord. Being made in God's image means not dominating any living creature. The old ideas of having dominion over the animals and subduing Earth have been rethought in this new story of cosmology. Being one with Earth, being of Earth, being "Earth in its conscious form" gives us a whole new perspective. If we are Earth come to consciousness (our very bodies, their organs, and fluids are all totally comprised of the very elements and interdependencies of the soil, air, water, and vegetation of the planet) then we would not desire to dominate Earth. Rather we would find great delight in freedom from domination and in receiving respect from others. That same freedom is what we desire for all.

To put away the concept of domination does not mean that we cannot use the gifts and resources of Earth. We are called to use them sparingly, taking reverently what we need to live simply, leaving for others what they need.

Another aspect of Christian tradition has been the emphasis on the incarnation, the word of God becoming one with human beings. Through this beautiful mystery of our faith we developed an anthropocentric sense, that is, that humans are the final aim of the universe and the only creatures through which the divine is revealed.

To gaze at a picture taken of planet Earth from outer space helps to put this into perspective. For in meditating on the divine mystery at the heart of the evolutionary process bringing Earth into being with such astonishing diversity and unity, we realize that the word of God, born of Mary, came through this same evolutionary process as all creation. We have all evolved from the same stuff—the same hydrogen, oxygen, carbon that were part of the beginnings of the evolutionary process.

So rather than focusing on the exclusive eminence of human beings "a new appreciation of and confidence in the earth is needed along with a capacity for communion with the earth. Only through communion can we have community. Only through an integral community can we survive." (Berry)

Perhaps this is what John Paul II had in mind when he called all women and men, and especially leaders, to a profound transformation in their accustomed ways of thinking and acting.

> Thus one would hope that all those who, to some degree or other, are responsible for ensuring a "more human life" for their fellow human beings, whether or not they are inspired by religious faith, will become fully aware of the urgent need to change the spiritual attitudes that define each individual's relationship with self, with neighbor, with even the remotest human communities and with nature itself. (*Sollicitudo Rei Socialis*)

To change our spiritual attitudes calls for conversion of heart. To change those spiritual attitudes that define our relationship with nature requires a shift in perception. This will require a new kind of learning, a disciplined study, and prayerful reflection that can lead us to a new understanding of our total unity with all creation. To do this alone may be difficult. For conversion usually requires helpers or a supportive community to listen to our story, to inspire us, to challenge us, to urge us on.

Cannot some of our helpers be the oceans, rivers, and streams, the forests, a live oak, the manatees, dolphins, other species that are endangered? Can we not listen to their stories and be their voice when we make decisions about our way of life which affects them so dramatically?

I hear a few voices in the Church telling the new sacred story of the universe but, by and large, I have not heard mention of the new story in our parish churches. Why? Have we forgotten that our Christian tradition holds that there are two scriptures: the scriptures of the natural world and the sacred scriptures of the Hebrew and Christian Bible? We have known this truth for centuries. Church authorities such as St. Thomas Aquinas, Doctor of the Church, in his *Summa Theologica* explained nature's powerful lessons. God speaks to us and is revealed to us through the natural world.

We can learn so much from reading the scriptures of the natural world. They reveal marvelous and mysterious dimensions about God and the laws upon which all life including our own depends. And it might be refreshing for parishioners to hear in homilies some of the wonders of the created world. Our mystics could be tapped and brought out of their hiding on bookshelves. Our poets and artists and musicians could incorporate the beauties of the natural world in our liturgies and rituals and concerts. We could ponder for a long time a statement such as this one from Ralph Waldo Emerson: "The creation of a thousand forests is in one acorn."

Or could we be inspired by the story told by Jean-Pierre Hallet who went into the Belgian Congo and discovered an elephant without a trunk. Knowing that the elephant cannot forage without a trunk he followed the elephant and his herd into the forest. There he saw the other elephants breaking off twigs and branches to feed the trunkless elephant. They were even vying with one another to gather the most food for their companion. They did all this without having eaten themselves. (Told by Eknath Easwaran in *The Compassionate Universe*.)

Stories like these will enrich us and give us food for thought. But we also must be about the telling of the great story, the universe story which tells why we are who we are, where we have come from, and leads us to a powerful realization that our present lifestyles, based on ever more consumption and disturbance of the natural world, cannot be sustained. We desperately need to correct our expectations of having and owning more. We need to see the simplicity of Jesus in a fresh new light.

To live simply means to live like the hummingbird which stops in flight for a split second and takes only the nectar it needs and in the process pollinates the flower. For too long we have been the takers, taking not only what we need but also what we think we need. True, we must not only survive but must also develop our deeper sensitivities for beauty and creativity, for knowledge and the full flowering of human potential. But today's culture says we are the clothes we wear, the car we drive, the possessions and power we acquire. Yet our addiction to consumerism and greed is tearing apart the fabric of Earth.

Now as I read and contemplate the universe story, I read not just from the point of view of learning history. I read with new eyes and new ears, with amazement and gratitude to Creator God for bringing forth a universe with all its wonders. I am in total awe of Earth teeming with magnificent creatures from eukaryotes to dinosaurs, from microbes to giraffes, from horseshoe crabs to humpback whales. I meditate on the ways in which each species has developed by adaptation to its setting and to the whole community of life to present us with such great differentiation and beauty.

As I learn how humans have evolved, I give praise for all that has gone before and pray that now we, who are Earth in its conscious form, will revel in the laws of nature which are also written in our hearts. These laws, differentiation, subjectivity and communion, are tendencies of nature revealed in the universe and in Earth.

Differentiation means that everything that is, is different from everything else that is. No two things in the universe are the same. Nature also informs us of subjectivity or interiority which means that each individual being is a subject not an object. Each existing thing carries its own uniqueness and interior mystery which is to be reverenced and honored.

And in the final law, communion, nature powerfully explains that everything and everyone is bound together. We are already in communion whether the human realizes it or not. But wouldn't it be wonderful if we all came to a deeper understanding of what it means to be in communion with the entire Earth system as well as with each other?

If these laws, finally discovered by our most sophisticated scientists, are the principles by which God has designed this incredible universe and this marvelous Earth, is it not imperative that our churches speak prophetically about our human responsibility to reverence and obey them?

Jesus taught us those three laws very simply when he said, "Love one another as I have loved you." Can we not extend that commandment to say, "Love one another and all creation as I have loved you"? We are called to be in communion with each other and all creation.

What the universe story teaches us is that this foundation of love, revealed by Jesus, must now be expanded to include, not only all the human community, but the entire community of the natural world and the universe itself.

Perhaps if we contemplated these laws or mysteries of the universe we might respond with alacrity to the devastation we have wrought on planet Earth. May it not be too late to save this splendid work of creation so that all the ways by which God has revealed the divine goodness may not be diminished and so that our children, grandchildren, and all living creatures will have a place to call home for a long, long time.

BIBLIOGRAPHY

Berry, Thomas. *The Dream of the Earth*. San Francisco: Sierra Club Books, 1988.

Berry, Thomas and Clark, Thomas. *Befriending the Earth*. Mystic: XXIII Publications, 1993.

Chardin, Teilhard de. *The Heart of the Matter*. New York: Harcourt Brace and Company, 1976.

Dowd, Michael. *Earthspirit*. Mystic: XXIII Publications, 1991.

Easwaran, Eknath. *The Compassionate Universe*. Petaluma, CA: Nilgiri Press, 1989.

Keller, Stephen and Wilson, Edwin O. *The Biophilia Hypothesis*. Washington, DC: Island Press, 1993.

Sahtouris, Elizabeth. *Gaia: The Human Journey from Chaos to Cosmos*. New York: Pocket Books, 1989.

Swimme, Brian. *The Universe Is a Green Dragon*. Santa Fe: Bear and Company, 1984.

Swimme, Brian and Berry, Thomas. *The Universe Story*. San Francisco: Harper, 1992.

11

Christ, the Church and Ministry:
A Theological Perspective

Edward J. Ciuba

If there is any one constant in Christian ministry, it is the constancy of *change*. Unquestionably, the last half of the twentieth century has witnessed more change in the theology and practice of the Catholic Church than was seen in the last four hundred years. But hasn't this always been so? Haven't changing times and circumstances always impacted on the nature of ministry?

Imagine yourself, for example, through some time warp, sitting at the feet of Jesus as he begins the Sermon on the Mount: "How blessed are the poor in spirit; the reign of God is theirs. Blessed too are the sorrowing; they shall be consoled. Blessed are they who hunger and thirst for holiness…" Captivated by these powerful and challenging words of Jesus, you recognize innately that following him will mean somehow enfleshing those attitudes into your own life. After all, continuing his mission is what ministry is all about.

Change the scenery then to the city of Rome about 165 A.D. Christians are being persecuted for their beliefs during the reign of the emperor Marcus Aurelius and are very much afraid for their lives. Your ministry in great part now involves finding hiding places for your hunted brothers and sisters in safe refuges throughout the city. Is this consistent with the tenets of the Galilean preacher of the previous century?

We move forward in time once again to Ireland of the fifth century A.D. You are now a part of that band of missionaries with St. Patrick who are instructing and baptizing the godless inhabitants of that emerald isle. Your ministry now is one of conversion to the Catholic faith and instructing heathen tribesmen in the tenets of the one, holy, catholic and apostolic church.

In the twelfth century A.D. you sail from Venice in the company of Godfrey of Boulogne and Richard the Lionhearted on extensive crusades to the Middle East to free the holy places from the hands of the infidels. Your ministry now involves the expulsion of infidels and the ransoming of Christian captives held in slavery. And all this in the name of God!

In the early sixteenth century A.D. you find yourself attracted to the charismatic preacher Martin Luther, who speaks to your heart about the need for reform in the Church. You find yourself forced to make a decision between the reformers of Luther and those who abide by the reigning pontiff. Your ministry now changes to giving aid to those embroiled in the religious/political wars that follow. A far cry from the Sermon on the Mount!

And finally, in the latter part of the nineteenth century you attach yourself to the Papal Zouaves protecting the Roman Pontiff and the Papal States against the anti-clerical forces of Garibaldi. Your ministry now includes taking up arms in defense of the Pope! Perhaps the historical examples are far-fetched. They do, however, point out that ministry is conditioned by changing times and circumstances.

In all ages, whatever the changing historical circumstances, valid Christian ministry must somehow continue the mission of Jesus Christ and his Church. Mission and ministry are always in close relationship with the Church and with Christ. "Ubi Christus, ibi Ecclesia." Where you find Christ, there too you will find his Church. In theological parlance, one's practical christology and ecclesiology will necessarily impact on the form and content of ministry. [1] It is becoming more clear to theologians and Church leaders that ecclesial issues will never be adequately resolved without a personal appropriation of Christ. Christology criticizes and determines ecclesiology, but not vice versa. [2]

Even ordinary decision-making that takes place in a parochial context bears this out. Consider, for example, a bi-monthly staff meeting that takes place in a contemporary parish. The issues discussed may include theological assumptions which will have a bearing on mission and ministry in that parish. For example, should the parish spend $50,000 on new liturgical renovations or hire a much-needed youth minister and secretary? Does the pastor disband the Parish Pastoral Council because they are too difficult to work with? Will the proceeds from the annual "Tricky Tray" Auction go toward funding scholarships for inner city students or for the renovation of the parish hall? Are women treated as equals and genuinely involved in the ministry of the parish? What levels of consultation are present?

Responses to such questions will have theological antecedents, whether they are recognized as such or not. When serious differences arise over these and similar parish issues, even in the context of genuine, honest dialogue, people will be heard to say: "Well, we obviously have different notions of Church!" Yes, differences do arise from different perceptions of Ecclesiology. But perhaps more significantly, though not always apparent, differences also arise because of different perceptions of Jesus Christ. It's the image of Jesus Christ that we appropriate into our faith lives that will impact on our understanding of Church, and, consequently, on our attitudes toward ministry. Furthermore, apropos of our times, when the major perception of Church and images of Christ begin to change, so also will perceptions of mission and ministry.

The aim of this essay then is to suggest the intimate relationship between Ministry, Ecclesiology and Christology. Very appropriately this essay honors Archbishop Peter L. Gerety, whose entire life has been steeped in ministry, in a faithful and abiding love of the Church and with deep personal commitment to Jesus Christ.

THE MISSION OF JESUS—THE MISSION OF THE CHURCH

Valid Christian ministry is a continuation of the ministry of Jesus. The function and mission of the Church, and thereby of all ministers of the Church, follows from the function and mission of Jesus. "The time is fulfilled; the reign of God is at hand. Repent and believe in the Gospel" are the opening words of Jesus as he begins his mission. (Mk 1:15) The presence of the "Reign of God" and the challenge to conversion or inner renewal of mind and heart on the part of hearers was much the same in Matthew and Luke. Through quaint, simple parable images and through the power of his miracles the Jesus of the Synoptic Gospels proclaimed the reality and possibilities of God's reign. The contemporary mission of the Church cannot be any other than a continuation of the mission of Jesus. Christian ministry is an expression of those who serve in the name of the Church and who are motivated by a deep faith and love of Jesus Christ.

Undoubtedly, there are many influences which impact on the nature of the Church and ministry. Political and social circumstances, historical and sociological, even psychological factors, all have some influence on the way men and women practice ministry in the Church. In this essay our purpose is to show how two significant theological factors, namely, Ecclesiology and Christology, influence the exercise of Christian ministry. In our changing times, when models of Church and images of Jesus Christ are shifting, so also in domino-like fashion will perceptions of ministry change.

In most instances, changes in the policies and programs of a parish, or even a diocese, respond to practical needs. They are done without formal theological reflection about their long term implications. Whenever a parish decides to make policy changes or programmatic innovations, it cannot be expected to undertake a major theological reflection to determine underlying theological assumptions about Church and Jesus Christ. Such assumptions may be implicit, if they are even recognized at all. Rare indeed would be the parish or diocese which would undertake planning by first asking itself questions like: "What is our prevailing model(s) of Church?" "What is the significant, personal image(s) of Jesus Christ that nurtures our perception of Church?" But, as a matter of fact, major new programs or policies that are undertaken in a parish will reveal a definite model(s) of Church and a certain image(s) of Jesus Christ, which will determine faith and practice. In other words, if form follows function, then the form and style of ministry will follow the function of Ecclesiology and Christology as understood by responsible authorities.

CHANGING MODELS OF CHURCH

To participate effectively in the Church's mission, one must possess an innate vision or perception of that reality called "Church," out of which and in whose name one ministers. Such a perception of Church may be inchoate, jejune, unclear or confused; it may be active or passive, conservative or progressive, systematic or functional. But it must exist in some form or shape, if valid ecclesial ministry is to take place.

The mission and ministry of Jesus Christ continues today in the Church, the Body of Christ, that community of faithful who testify in word and deed to the ongoing Spirit of Jesus. If mission and ministry are a form and function of the Church, then as the model of Church changes, so also will the forms and functions of ministry begin to change.

Even before Vatican Council II, the traditional institutional model of Church, which had endured over the previous four hundred years, was being perceived differently. In Pius XII's encyclical of 1950, *Mystici Corporis*, the notion of the Church as a "Mystical Body" was dramatically different from the idea of the Church as a "perfect society," as conceived by Cardinal Bellarmine a century before.[3] But it was the pastoral orientation of Vatican II, so clearly enunciated in the Constitution on the Church (*Lumen Gentium*) and the Constitution on the Church in the Modern World (*Gaudium et Spes*), that gave rise to a variety of different Church images with strong biblical roots. Re-imaging the Church as the People of God, Body of Christ, Sacrament, Communion, Servant, led to obvious departures from a previous perception of the Church as a "perfect society." Given the major changes that were taking place in society, the autonomous, self-sufficient institutional model of Church was inadequate.

The opening paragraph of *Lumen Gentium* pointed to a new approach in understanding Church. "The Church is a *sacrament* or *sign* of salvation."[4] To speak of a sign or sacrament meant putting aside an older point of view of the Church as a sanctuary of salvation, a repository of truth, a perfect society. Sacrament points beyond itself; it is open to the world rather than being turned inward defensively. It discloses rather than encloses; it represents the love of Christ to the world. It speaks about conversion of heart and mind rather than conversion to a Church body. A seemingly small shift from viewing the Church as sacrament rather than institution has far reaching consequences for mission.[5]

Once there is a shift from an institutional model to that of sign/sacrament, inevitably changes will take place in the understanding of mission and ministry. In a parish context the most important work will be that of giving *witness*. The Church is clearly apparent as sacrament when its members are united to one another and to God through holiness and mutual love. The sign aspect is most evident in Eucharistic celebration. It actualizes Christ's presence in ritual signs. It binds community together with God in Christ and through the Holy Spirit with one another. It is indivisibly christological and ecclesiological. From a sign perspective, mission will be seen no more as conversion to a body which possesses the fullness of truth or a "perfect society." Instead, mission and ministry will strive to make credible the genuine witness of holiness in the lives of its members. The model of Church as sign/sacrament has strong roots in Sacred Scripture. It is less juridical, less clerical, less triumphalistic. It is more ecumenical, charismatic and collegial. Ministry and ministers will shift accordingly.

One of the most highly regarded images of Church today is that of "communion." In the words of the bishops convened by Pope John Paul II in Universal Synod (Rome, 1985), "The ecclesiology of communion is the central and fundamental idea in the documents of the Council....it is the foundation for order in the Church, and especially, for a correct relationship in the unity and diversity of the church."[6] With the image of the Church as "communion" comes the profound awareness that all the baptized are animated by the Spirit of God. In a parochial setting the most important work will be the formation of a genuine sense of "community," making all aware of their empowerment by the Holy Spirit. Ministry will involve making people more conscious of their gifts to be used in continuing Christ's mission. Ministry becomes more collaborative, more collegial, more aware of the various gifts that can be used for the common good. A priest will see himself, for example, as an orchestra conductor, instead of trying to do the work of the entire orchestra. The development of lay leadership becomes one of the major goals of "communion" Church. The collaborative activity of clergy and laypeople working together in common mission becomes very much a part and parcel of the communion model of Church.

The Church as "Servant," on the other hand, includes in its mission the struggle for peace and justice, the concern for the poor and the downtrodden, a sensitivity beyond word and sacrament to include a wider social, economic and political agenda. The Servant model of Church will strive to incorporate in its mission the words of the 1971 World Synod of Bishops: "Action on behalf of justice and participation in the transformation of the world appears to us as a constitutive dimension of the preaching of the Gospel."[7] With such an ecclesiological vision the most important work of the parish will be to care for people who are in genuine need of help and to address these systems and structures that make for poverty. The strength of its mission and ministry will depend on how well it becomes aware of and responds to the areas of injustice in the community and the world at large.

With the Church as "Herald" the vital mission of ministers will be the study of the Scriptures and a genuine desire to live by its principles. Important avenues of ministry will include the formation of Bible study groups, scriptural prayer groups and the formation of small faith sharing communities.

Obviously, models of Church are never meant to be exclusive and interdependent. They do not exist as separate entities. There is inevitably an overlap. Avery Dulles, who has popularized the notion of Church models and their ramifications, has been the first to point out the intermixture of Church models.[8] The different models are like intersecting circles—or they should be. The models of Church as Communion and Servant, for example, are well founded in tradition. But they can never be fully disconnected from the institutional model. Vatican II's Constitution on the Church did much to rectify a model of Church that was being perceived as too institutional. With each shift or adjustment in the model of Church that is perceived and appropriated, there will also be shifts in the understanding of ministry as well as the roles and functions of ministers in the Church.

REBIRTH IN CHRISTOLOGY: DEFFERENT IMAGES OF CHRIST

As new models of Church have arisen in the light of Vatican II, so also have new images of Jesus Christ come to the forefront. The volume and vigor of christological studies over the last few decades comes as a logical consequence of new insights into the nature of the Church. In logical order, when theological assumptions of Ecclesiology and Christology are reflected upon they will inevitably have an impact on ministry and ministerial formation. However, at the front and center of reflection on the Church, its mission and ministers is the image of Jesus Christ. How does one's personal appropriation of the meaning of Jesus Christ impact on ministry and ministerial life?

A revitalized Christology provides the cornerstone for identity and formation of church ministers in changing times and circumstances. Although theological literature on the identity, nature and person of Jesus Christ has grown by leaps and bounds over the last three decades, what is needed is a *practical* and *functional* Christology. Not merely is it the question: "Who do you say that I am?" or "What is the nature of Jesus?" that must be asked. More significant for ministry is: "What meaning does Jesus Christ have in your life?" Sadly, so much of Christology is disengaged from Soteriology. But knowing Christ in himself is incomplete, unless we also know him as Savior for *us*. Jesus' followers in the New Testament first believed that he was the primary revelation of God. Jesus came to save them. Only afterwards did the tradition of the Church inquire about his identity and nature. The experience of salvation precedes inquiry into the nature of Jesus' identity. The same holds true for us.

A practical, functional Christology must be rooted in an image(s) of the historical Jesus that can be easily enfleshed in those who are once again called to be a part of his mission. Where personal reflection on the meaning of Jesus Christ is lacking, ministry is impoverished and ministerial identity suffers. The same holds true for the Christian community. Where a traditional and long-standing operative Christology no longer invites, attracts, challenges and excites members of a faith community, faith wanes, love diminishes and ministry dies.

Two significant factors have contributed to the development of new images of Christ that have bearing on the Christian community:

1. the major impact of scriptural scholarship over the last half century, and
2. a growing awareness of the limitations of the traditional Chalcedonian formula of Jesus Christ, the Second Person of the Blessed Trinity, as a model for ministry.

Recent Gospel scholarship, for example, has resulted in a growing mass of literature on the different portraits of Jesus. Not only do the Gospels reveal different portraits of Jesus, but critical methods of interpretation can actually pinpoint the significant shifts and changes in the organic process leading to the final completed portrait.[9] The various portraits of Christ are influenced by the real-life experience and pastoral needs of the community for whom the evangelists write. In turn, that completed image of Christ will impact on the faith and ministry of that community to which it is directed. The task of translating a Christ image from the past into present day categories goes on constantly. Hermeneutics, or the art and process of communicating the message from the past to the present, is never finished. Ministry will always be influenced by one's image of Christ.

Furthermore, the long-standing Chalcedonian formula for Jesus as God Incarnate, One Person with two natures, existing from eternity in the divine nature and becoming man at a certain time and point in history, is beginning to show the wear and tear of time. Theologically it is durable; functionally however it is not dynamic enough. It is too philosophical; it lacks the historical, human and experiential dimensions. In addition, the concepts of person and nature are being understood differently today.

The major shift in contemporary Christology begins with an examination and appropriation of the real earthly, historical experience of Jesus. Corresponding to the testimony of the Gospels, there is a strong desire to begin, like the first disciples, with the human Jesus. This "Christology from below" begins with the historical experience of Jesus as Proclaimer of the Reign of God, Prophet, Teacher of Parables, Merciful and Compassionate Healer. It begins "from below," from historical experience. In fact, it is the only one we can begin with.

Such imaging of Jesus gives rise to contemporary portraits of Jesus as Liberator of the Downtrodden, Man of God for Others, Human Face of God, Compassionate Healer, Brother in the Spirit, etc.[10]

The more traditional Christology "from above" emphasizes the Incarnation. Divinity and Humanity come together, without losing their separateness, in the Word made flesh. The key feature about Jesus is that he is divine. He is God's Son. The focus is on the sacred, the supernatural, the higher calling, the apartness from the world, the special vocation.

These two dimensions of Christology cannot be separated. They are not in conflict. Even with the contemporary emphasis on the historical, earthly, human Christology "from below," there is no intention of pitting one against the other. For a correct understanding of Jesus Christ, both dimensions must be recognized.

A shift in a person's consciousness of Jesus Christ will inevitably have an impact on one's understanding of Church, as well as on mission and ministry. Those who exercise ministry today will have different perceptions of Church resulting from their practical Christology. There is no question that the intimate relationship between Christ and Church as personally appropriated in the life of people in ministry today will affect their actions. It does appear that traditional models based on a "Christology from above" are losing some of their vitality and are giving way to scripturally-based, more experiential models more in keeping with the pastoral needs of ministry today.

CONSEQUENCES FOR MINISTRY

Unquestionably, a vital interaction exists between Christology, Ecclesiology, Mission and Ministry. The way we understand Jesus Christ as a vital factor in our faith will impact on our understanding of the meaning of Church. This perception in turn will impact on our view of ministry and the manner in which Church ministers perform. A shift in image perception will have repercussions down the line. In most instances those who are involved in the ministry of the Church do not consciously reflect on such theological perceptions of the Church and Christ before they undertake plans and programs in their mission and ministry. Perhaps they should. Most often these concepts of Church and Christ simply become a part of our day-to-day spirituality. Our spiritual lives do, in fact, impact on our ministry in a very real way. We have christological and ecclesiological perceptions without knowing about them.

Even with the challenges involved in bringing parish staffs or even a diocesan staff to such reflection, a clearer focus would be established for the future.

The consequences of shifting Christologies and Ecclesiologies are both negative and positive. Negatively, a pluriformity of different images of Christ and the Church can lead to confusion, a blurring of the clear focus given by one identifiable image. When paradigms begin to change, so does clarity or vision. Understandably, mission becomes more difficult when there is no one clear image to motivate, when there are too many images for a clear focus. Perhaps one of the reasons for the decline in vocations to the priesthood and religious life in the Church today is the confusion of many images of Christ. In prior times there was one central image of Jesus, the Son of God, the Great High Priest. The institutional image of the Church was clear. It provided strength and security. There was similarity of liturgical language (Latin), unity in doctrine, discipline and even attire. With the change in models and images, these become less important. But there is also less clarity.

On the other hand, the variety of images of Christ and models of Church can lead to greater richness and creativity in ministry. Pluriformity also does have its advantages. The different Gospel images of Jesus Christ respect more the individuality of different personalities who are responding. Not everyone has to conform to the same image; not everyone has to be bent into the same shape and mold. Uniformity can become stifling. Pluriformity of models allows for more flexibility and resiliency.

It also allows us to recognize that there is something in all of the images of Jesus and models of the Church that has value. Unilateral models tend toward exclusivity. Pluriformity helps us to appreciate that different pastoral needs and circumstances will call forth different perceptions of Jesus and the Church. Such was the situation in the communities of the New Testament. The pastoral needs and experiences of a given faith-community called forth different images of Christ and Church, different ministerial responses. The Church of Newark will call forth different ministerial responses than parishes in suburbia. There is one faith, one Lord, one baptism, but different responses as the Spirit calls.

Lastly, pluriformity of images of Jesus Christ challenges each and every one personally to identify that image which most accords with our spiritual life. We are all different personalities. But what image of Jesus Christ animates our lives and actions, motivates us, gives us focus and direction? What image makes our lives tolerable and challenges us to do what we are called upon to do in ministry? The way we perceive and appropriate the meaning of Jesus Christ will touch us differently. When there is a pluriformity of images, we are challenged to choose. If we are in ministry, we cannot not choose. We will respond differently. The question is: which image(s) of Jesus Christ affects my life profoundly? When we can clearly answer that question, we shall also recognize our model of Church, the direction of our mission and the manner in which we will exercise our ministry.

Endnotes

1. Peter J. Schineller, S.J., "Christ and Church: A Spectrum of Views," *Theological Studies* 37 (1976) 545–566.

2. Gerald, O'Collins, S.J. *What Are They Saying About Jesus?* (New York: Paulist Press, 1977) 29; cf. also Cardinal Joseph L. Bernardin, "The Future of Church and Ministry," *Origins*, Vol. II, No. 47 (May 6, 1982) 748.

3. E. Mersch, *The Theology of the Mystical Body*, English translation (St. Louis, MO.: B. Herder, 1951); A. Dulles, S.J., "A Half Century of Ecclesiology," *Theological Studies* 50, 3 (1989) 421–425.

4. The Constitution on the Church of Vatican II (*Lumen Gentium*), No. 48, par. 2, 79 in *The Documents of Vatican II*, Walter Abbott, S.J., ed. (New York: Herder & Herder, 1966).

5. William B. Frazier, M.M., "Guidelines for a New Theology of Mission" Address given to the Directors of the Society of the Propagation of the Faith (Chicago, Nov. 8, 1967) 5.

6. Text of the Final Report Adopted by the Synod of Bishops in Rome, Par. C, "Church as Communion" (*N.Y. Times*; Dec. 8, 1985) p. 34.

7. *Justice in the World* (1971 World Synod of Bishops).

8. Avery, Dulles, S.J., *Models of the Church* (N.Y.: Doubleday, 1974).

9. Jerome H. Neyrey, S.J., *Christ Is Community: The Christologies of the New Testament* (Wilmington: Glazier, 1985) 276.

10. John F. O'Grady, *Models of Jesus* (N.Y.: Doubleday Image Book, 1982).

12

Vignettes I, II and III

Edgar Holden, O.F.M. Conv.

VIGNETTE #I: PETER OR PAUL?

The winters at St. Anthony-on-Hudson in upstate New York were long and very cold ones. But all through my years of striving to impart the rudiments of systematic theology to the chilled and "huddled masses" of friars, there was always a happy and longed-for reward that lay ahead.

The prize? Spending two weeks of thawing out each August in the warm sun of York Beach, Maine. Those were the late 1960's and early 1970's.

The two-mile walk from the Nubble Light House area to St. Mary, Star of the Sea parish church was, as Maine vacationers stylishly called it, enchanting. One trouble was that, before Mass each Sunday, I'd always seem to be asking the pastor the first name of the presiding bishop of the Diocese of Portland in order to include it in the Commemoration of the Living. The fact of the matter was that the name, Peter Leo Gerety, never dug deep in my memory. With all due respect, I suppose I'd be thinking, "What has he brought about in the ecclesial world that I should remember his name from one summer to the next?"

I do recall celebrating the 9:00 A.M. Liturgy one Sunday at St. Mary's that caught the attention of the pastor. While he was waiting in the sacristy to assist with the distribution of Holy Communion, he over-heard me intoning: "Lord, remember your Church throughout the world; make us grow in love with Paul, our Pope, and—uh, let's see now—oh, yes, *Paul* our bishop, and all the clergy." After Mass the pastor gently reminded me that, while here in Maine, it might help if I'd strive to recall at Mass the names of the great apostles, Peter and Paul.

"Now, if you can make an effort to remember that *Paul* is our reigning pontiff, it rather follows that the other illustrious name, *Peter*, is that of our bishop. It's truly not an arduous task if you set your mind to it."

Another spirited memory of my York Beach days related to the weekly Catholic newspaper of the Diocese of Portland. The paper's name escapes me, as does that of the editor, but he was a layman. In those heady days following Vatican Council II, most diocesan publications reflected a new confidence. At the same time, the specter of the pre-Vatican II era of censorship was not altogether banished from the memories of most editors throughout America. Such clearly was *not* the case as it related to Portland's diocesan weekly. Not only was the editor forthright in addressing the cogent and controversial issues of that era but, as well, the spirit of a free press in its best sense was reflected throughout its pages. Portland's Catholic weekly enlivened its readership by being on the cutting edge of things. Simply put, it was an unusually excellent diocesan newspaper. Whether it ever garnered awards from the Catholic Press Association, we're unaware. But if it didn't, it should have.

Anent this subject, I can remember musing that such journalistic forthrightness simply doesn't come about in an official diocesan journal without the behind-the-scene backing of a benign and forward-thinking prelate. It became quite clear to the discerning reader that the presiding Bishop of Portland had to be a prelate who was determined to disseminate the fresh air that Pope John XXIII desired to be blown throughout all of Christendom. And it was likewise clear that he, Peter Leo Gerety, a prelate of unusual credentials, was not long for the Pine Tree State.

Moving along, I quite forget whether high officials at the Vatican sought my advice directly. But it was obvious that the "Biggies" over there had somehow tapped into my thought processes. For, sure enough, Portland's bishop was soon asked to step into a position of authority that only a cleric of substantial credentials would be qualified to undertake. The gentleman in question was named the Archbishop of Newark on April 2, 1974.

Well, the newly-designated archbishop was now out of my life. He resided in Newark, N.J., and I in Rensselaer, N.Y. This friar continued his two-week summering stint at York Beach each year. And, truth to tell, it became somewhat easier at Mass to remember the name of the new bishop, Edward C. O'Leary, than that of his predecessor. That

Peter and Paul thing was always—well, confusing. Too apostolic. Too authoritarian. And too alliterative.

Little did I know at the time that five of the happiest of the fifty years of my priesthood would soon find me in the Archdiocese of Newark. Its benign prelate wanted to initiate an heretofore unmentionable outreach to a group of very hurting souls.

VIGNETTE II: "THOSE PEOPLE"

The middle 1970's were good years for a lot of people. It was generally a demoralizing era, however, for separated and divorced Catholics. At best, these fellow Christians were viewed somewhat as a group apart. At worst? Well, we'll let that slide.

Suffice it to say that many otherwise enlightened Christians, both cleric and lay, often referred to Catholics in concluded marriages as "those people." Doesn't that say something?

About this time, a ripple-making prelate from Maine appeared on the scene in Newark. This new archbishop, Peter Leo Gerety, set many things in motion. One of his enterprises took good guts: he instituted an *official* office in the archdiocese for those in disrupted marriages. Many of these, the divorced, the separated and those who had married again irregularly, had long since separated themselves from the institutional Church. They felt there was no place therein for them or for their children.

Looking back, it must be remembered that, up until 1977 in our American church (and *only* in our American church), divorced Catholics who had married without the benefit of a Declaration of Nullity fell under the penalty of *excommunication*. Other divorced but non-excommunicated Catholics tried sheepishly to hang in with their Church, attempting to hold their heads reasonably high. But it wasn't easy for them or for their children.

Again, a point to recall is that, up to that "Gerety moment" in North American Catholicism, no prelate had programmed an outreach to separated, divorced and remarried Catholics as an official agency of a diocese. It simply wasn't done. Peter L. Gerety did! The year was 1975. It was called Ministry to Divorced Catholics (MDC).

Let something be immediately said: Looking back from the vantage point of 1996, many thousands of "those people," long estranged in one degree or another from Mother Church, are now walking around the

Archdiocese of Newark as happy, heads-held-high, practicing Catholics and quick on the draw to own up to their affiliation. And of equal or possibly greater importance, *so are their children.*

We now muse over the evolution of MDC. This newly-established outreach didn't get off to an easy start during its first month. MDC's first meeting, heralded in *The Advocate,* was held at St. Leo's Church, Irvington, N.J. on an October evening in 1975. Few attended. Those brave souls who did were chary and frightened. The fact that *The Advocate's* photographer later complained that he couldn't get any front-face shots of those present points up the camera-shyness of "those people."

The November meeting of 1975, however, was infinitely more encouraging. Two factors brought this about: (1) The word had spread like magic throughout Essex and Union counties that "the Church *really* cares about us." And (2) the well-publicized speaker of the evening was to be the gentle, scholarly and lovable clergyman, Father Leo Farley. Despite a torrential rainstorm throughout the entire evening, the hall was filled to capacity with active and inactive Catholics of many descriptions, all looking and hoping and asking, "Do we still have a chance of making it in our Church?"

And our answer was, "Boy, do you!" Even the ladies didn't mind the chauvinistic response. Would that we could have anticipated the words of Pope John Paul II in his *Apostolic Exhortation on the Family* (Dec. 15, 1981). How comforting the Pontiff's words would have been to those who had remarried civilly. Our Holy Father wrote:

> Finally, there are those who have entered a second union and who are sometimes subjectively certain in conscience that their previous and irreparably destroyed marriage had never been valid. Together with the Synod, I earnestly call upon pastors and the whole community of the faithful to help the divorced and with solicitous care to make sure they *do not consider themselves as separated from the church* (emphasis added). Let the church pray for them, encourage them and show herself a merciful mother and thus sustain them in faith and hope. (Cf. *Origins,* Vol. 11, Nos. 28 & 29, p. 465)

The Ministry to Divorced Catholics in the Archdiocese of Newark "took off" as the saying has it. After that rather memorable November, 1975, meeting in Irvington, MDC soon found its way into parish life of Essex, Union, Bergen and Hudson counties. Apart from the major role that *The Advocate* played in MDC's growth, the ministry was accorded equally generous exposure in parish bulletins and the secular press of northern New Jersey and New York City. The MDC office was accorded numerous invitations to "explain itself" to viewers of television in the Greater New York area. New York's Channel 13, in fact, did a five-day prime-time series on MDC that brought a volume of mail and phone calls that taxed our office for days thereafter. The unexpected response caused MDC's two secretaries to remark with a note of fear in their voices, "What kind of monster have we let loose?"

And, as always, practically every inquirer posed the same question: "Is there still hope for us in the Catholic Church?" And, as always, our response was. "As long as there's a God above, there'll be hope for you in the Catholic Church." As an aside, we found the most lethal enemies of our ministry were those who enjoyed standing in judgment of others, especially those whose minds and hearts were full of condemning feelings toward the separated and divorced. We thought this particularly strange inasmuch as, more often than not, one of the parties in a concluded marriage did not want the separation to come about in the first place. Why, then, should he or she be looked upon as a pariah? Where is the sin?

In this whole area of human frailty, we used the following as our rule of thumb: "If you're God, *judge.* If you're not God but like to think you are, *don't* judge. And finally, if you're not God and know you're not, *thank* God!"

The Ministry to Divorced Catholics in the Archdiocese of Newark became a broad pathway for many to return to their Church. This would not have come about had it not been for the loving concern of the archdiocese's vicar-bishops, priests, religious and laity.

But it took the vision and caring and deep love of one person to put the whole thing in motion: his initials, P.L.G.

A divorced friend of this writer once observed, "Our archbishop is one helluva man." Rather inelegantly phrased, no doubt, but surely on target.

As for this writer, he'll always remember Archbishop Peter L. Gerety as the best friend "those people" ever had.

VIGNETTE III: A SECOND FIRST COMMUNION*

It was a hot, soggy evening as I entered the hospital. An anonymous letter received the previous day had clarified my mission: I was to see

Mike Sullivan (not his real name) in Room 518; he was seriously ill. In addition, he was a divorced Catholic who many years ago married "outside the church." Although we had never met, it was my appointed task to straighten him out with the church. Just like that? At least that's what the letter writer suggested.

The information proved somewhat inaccurate. He wasn't in Room 518, but in Intensive Care. And I was assured Mike was more than seriously ill: he was dying. It was his heart.

Entering the two-bed unit, I wondered which patient was mine. One reminded me of an astronaut strapped and wired into his take-off contraption. It turned out to be Mike. About 45 years old, he was a muscular six-footer. Above his head was a monitoring machine. It was indecipherable what the monitor was saying, but, I'll tell you, it was doing some fancy dancing.

"Hi, Mike. You don't know me. My name is Ed Holden. As you can see, I'm a priest." His facial expression didn't change one line. "If you weren't confined to this bed," I added, "I'd like to see you playing defensive tackle with the Washington Redskins. They could use you."

That bit of whimsy evinced but the merest suggestion of a smile. He was playing this cool, no doubt about it. All the while I'm side-glancing at the jittery monitor that was bugging me out of my Thom McAns. "If my information is correct, good friend, we have something in common. You're a divorced and remarried Catholic, and my full-time privilege is working with divorced Catholics." Then in carefully measured words, I said, "I'm here to say that God loves you. He loves you very much."

Again, his momentary reaction was an expressionless silence. Not for long. He sucked in a long draft of air, held his breath and then let loose, with tears. Buckets of them.

Dear Lord, I'm thinking, why did I raise the issue so abruptly? What will the monitor say? And the fellow in the next bed? How about the hospital people—will they suggest I volunteer for a tour of duty in El Salvador?

Big Mike just kept weeping. And Little Ed stood there like Padre El Dumbo. It took a couple of minutes for things to quiet down. When they did, he raised his hand. Mike wanted to hold mine, no, squeeze mine. Notwithstanding his bad heart, his grip was something that John McEnroe would envy. Mike wasn't talking yet, but in that moment of squeezing, I knew God was moving in. His eyes began twinkling. Even the rude monitor seemed less clinical. Really, the instant called for a little to be said. Silence was articulating eloquently. Looking back, I did want to whisper, "Ouch!" He was sort of mashing the uncrushed bones in my right hand. My ordination fingers, I fretted. Being thrown to the lions could have been worse, I consoled myself.

Mike cleared his throat. "Are you telling me I can be a Catholic again?" he asked. "If 'Catholic' means loving God, I'm saying you never stopped being one." It was then I noticed a battered prayerbook on his nightstand. Next to it rested rosary beads whose decades had seen better ones.

"Let's talk, Mike, just a little bit." It was at this point that he released his grip on my hand. Bless him, Lord, I sighed under my breath. "On second thought, let me do the talking," I insisted. "Your case, facts unknown, would be easy to unfold. Wanna bet? Just stop me when I'm wrong."

The pattern seldom changes. Born, reared and educated in the Catholic faith, he married at a teenish age. It was a church wedding with all the ethnic trimmings. The whole thing came to a crashing halt 20 months later. Predictably so. Whose fault it was, if either's, doesn't really matter here. Each was ridiculously ill-equipped at that time to confront the grave responsibilities they assumed. That better people could do so only proves that there were better people out there. Those two couldn't. So they separated. He didn't know what became of her after the divorce. He remarried several years later. "I now have a loving wife and four beautiful children," he confided softly.

Yes, he had submitted his case to the diocese's matrimonial tribunal before his second marriage. He was told "no." That was standard practice in those good old rotten tribunal days.

"We're raising our children as strict Catholics, Father," Mike said. (It was the first time he'd called me Father.) "My wife goes to Mass but not to Communion. I don't go to church at all. (Pause #1.) I can't. It hurts too much. (Pause #2.) I can't stand the memories and all the guilt. (Big pause #3.) I've been pretty lousy to God. Why do you say He loves me?" Niagara Falls revisited. Yep, the tears. Honest, big, decent, God-fearing, God-loving tears. He bawled himself out.

About a half-box of Kleenex later, I said: "Listen, Mike, I'm leaving you for about 10 minutes. When I return, I'm sure you'll want to go to Confession. We're calling it Reconciliation these days. No matter. You're going to be absolved from every sin you ever committed—tiny sins, giant economy-size sins, any you've ever forgotten, sins you may have been ashamed to confess, any Church laws you've broken. Everything! This is the way God wants it. And I don't want to hear that you're not worthy. By that reasoning, all of us are unworthy—my sainted mother, Pope John Paul, and let's throw in Mother Teresa for good luck. I'll be seeing you in 10 minutes."

Out in the lobby I flopped into a big soft chair. My emotions alternated between seething and being ashamed of myself. I seethed at the Church I was born in and the Church I'll happily die in. Our Lord, I fulminated, wouldn't be caught in the same room—any room!—with some of the unfeeling, soul-crushing, religion-killing, credibility-destroying man-made laws and practices in our Church's grab-bag. And I felt ashamed that I, a priest, was expected to stand behind and even enforce some of this highly questionable practice, especially the disciplinary laws governing marriage. Talk about man being made for the Sabbath!

My petulance behind me, I bounced back into Mike's room. Darned if he wasn't smiling. After another five minutes he had even more reason to smile. He availed himself of the privilege, too. By now hospital authorities had summoned his wife. Her arrival was perfectly timed. To the degree that I could, I briefed her and her two daughters. I then departed in order to bring back the Blessed Eucharist. "I'll be returning in a jiffy. Don't have any fun without me," I warned.

The wife and daughters knelt down upon my return. The familiar old prayers from the ritual were read slowly. I suspect they held newer meaning for Mike. Eyes alert, he listened carefully, absorbing every word like a blotter. I had explained the optional manner of receiving the Eucharist. He extended cupped hands. A few more prayers were read.

Then a bit of silence. The elder daughter broke the ice: "Daddy, lucky you. This is your second first Holy Communion. I guess you're expecting a gift? Well, here's one." She kissed him and the other two followed suit. Lovingly. And the guy didn't even shed a tear! These tough bruisers are hard to figure.

It was rather late by the time the doctor pronounced what he had to pronounce. I took a last look at the crazy monitor. It had ceased its activity, of course, as though it, too, wanted to pay respect to a guy with a big heart. The old prayerbook and beads remained on the nightstand as I left the room.

It was still hot and sticky as I walked out into the night. The gratitude I owed that anonymous letter writer occupied my thoughts. Groping my way to the parking lot, I found my car and got in. Everything was uncomfortably quiet. Spooky. I decided to make some noise. So I sat back and cried.

*Editor's note: This article, authored by Edgar Holden, first appeared in *America* (Oct. 17, 1981). It has since been reprinted in over 75 secular and religious publications.

Editor's Postscript

My own fortunate and very happy association with Archbishop Gerety goes back to his first years at Newark. I was then at CARA in Washington. We did many studies and worked on a number of programs. But none were as joyful, as challenging, and as fruitful as the work with Monsignor Thomas Kleissler and with Monsignor Thomas Ivory on developing and initiating RENEW.

One day not long ago Tom and Tom and I were reflecting on all this when spontaneously we said, "We should do something to honor our dear friend!" We did.

And the moment we requested contributors, the response was enthusiastic and energetic. We could have had a dozen more.

The very first response was from Bishop Joseph Francis, SVD. Our dear friends Cardinal Bernardin and Archbishop McCarrick so graciously and willingly contributed the Preface and Foreword.

To all those who contributed not only the excellent articles but in so many ways, and especially my secretaries, Dorothy Armstrong and Joan Santoriello, Tom and Tom and I are most grateful.

In a very special way a debt of gratitude is owed to Monsignor Kleissler and Monsignor Ivory without whom you would not have this book in your hands.

Cassian J. Yuhaus, C.P.

Contributors

Preface

His Eminence, JOSEPH CARDINAL BERNARDIN, D.D. is Cardinal Archbishop of Chicago, Illinois.

Foreword

Archbishop THEODORE E. McCARRICK, PH.D., D.D. is Archbishop of Newark, New Jersey.

An Archbishop for Our Time

MONSIGNOR FRANKLYN M. CASALE is President of St. Thomas University in Miami, Florida. He is a priest of the Archdiocese of Newark, ordained in 1967. Msgr. Casale served as an associate pastor and pastor in the Newark Archdiocese. He served as secretary, chancellor and Moderator of the Curia of the Archdiocese of Newark under Most Rev. Peter Leo Gerety, and was Vicar General for Public Affairs of the Archdiocese of Newark under Most Rev. Theodore E. McCarrick, Archbishop of Newark. Monsignor Casale has degrees from Seton Hall University, Catholic University of America and Immaculate Conception Seminary.

Christ, the Church and Ministry: A Theological Perspective

REV. MSGR. EDWARD J. CIUBA is presently pastor of Notre Dame Church in North Caldwell, N.J. A former professor of Sacred Scripture at Immaculate Conception Seminary (Darlington), Msgr. Ciuba was also appointed Rector of the Seminary by Archbishop

Peter L. Gerety. He continued in that capacity from 1974 to 1985, before the Seminary was relocated to the campus of Seton Hall University in South Orange, N.J. He received a Licentiate in Sacred Theology from the Gregorian University in Rome (1955–59), and then a Licentiate in Sacred Scripture from the Pontifical Biblical Institute in Rome (1960–62). He was awarded the certificate "Eleve Titulaire" of the Ecole Biblique in Jerusalem (1963). His book, *"Who Do You Say That I Am?" An Adult Inquiry into the First Three Gospels*, has undergone a new major revision (Staten Island: Alba House, 1991).

A New and Intense World of Ministry

BISHOP JOSEPH ABEL FRANCIS, S.V.D., D.D. is Auxiliary Bishop of Newark. Ordained Bishop by Archbishop Peter Leo Gerety, D.D. on June 26, 1976 he served with the Archbishop until the latter's retirement. Bishop Francis has very extensive educational, pastoral and administrative experience. He is the founder, and was first principal, of Verbum Dei High School, Watts, California; Provincial Superior of both the Western and then Southern Province of the Divine Word Fathers; past President of the Conference of Major Superiors of Men and of the National Office for Black Catholics; past Chairman of the Greater Newark Urban Coalition. Bishop Francis has served on a large number of Boards, civic and religious. He is one of the best known Bishops of the United States, and has lectured extensively in the United States, Canada and abroad. Among his many awards is "Principal Architect of the Pastoral for Interracial Justice," conferred by the National Conference for Urban Justice.

Vignettes I, II and III

Conventual Franciscan FATHER EDGAR HOLDEN, a native of Washington, D.C., was ordained to the priesthood Jan. 13, 1945. After receiving a Doctorate in Theology in 1947 from the University of Montreal, he was professor of Systematic Theology at St. Anthony-on-Hudson from 1947 to 1960. Designated by his community as foreign mission procurator from 1960 to 1970, this assignment took him into over eighty-five countries on five Continents. His next two assignments were at CARA from 1970 to 1972, and to the United

States Catholic Conference from 1972 to 1975 as Director of Development for the Division of Latin America. An invitation from Archbishop Gerety to initiate a Ministry to Divorced Catholics in the Archdiocese of Newark was joyfully accepted. This five-year term concluded in 1980. His Franciscan superiors again assigned him to foreign mission procurating until 1987. Receiving his very first parish assignment to Our Lady of Fatima Chapel, Winston-Salem, N.C., in 1987, Father Edgar is now in semi-retirement in Winston-Salem. He observed recently: "This semi-retirement is a killer. There's no time to rest!"

Dear Archbishop

DORIS HUDSON has lived in the Archdiocese of Newark all her life. For thirty-eight years she was married to her beloved Al who died in August of 1994. She is the mother of three children and the grandmother of four grandsons. Doris was an elected member and officer of the NCCB/USCC Advisory Council from 1975–1977. In the diocese, she worked and lectured on shared responsibility and spiritual renewal. In the parish she served as a Eucharistic Minister, leader of song, in RCIA and in the formation of small parish communities. As an adjunct instructor in Immaculate Conception Seminary she taught behavioral science and women's studies. She is presently teaching history and Latin in Glen Ridge High School from which she will retire in June and move to the Jersey shore.

Priestly Spirituality: Then and Now

JOHN JAY HUGHES is a widely published Church historian and a priest of the Archdiocese of St. Louis. He has taught at universities on both sides of the Atlantic, served as pastor of three parishes, and worked in diocesan administration. He is the author of nine books and numerous articles, and serves as a theological consultant.

A Pastoral Vision

MONSIGNOR THOMAS P. IVORY is pastor of Ascension Parish, New Milford, N.J. He has served as Spiritual Director and Rector of the American College, Louvain, Belgium where he earned his doctorate in Theology in 1976. He served on the staff of Archbishop Peter L. Gerety, D.D. as Archdiocesan Director of Religious Education and as Assistant Chancellor for Pastoral Services. He is past president of the National Conference of Diocesan Directors of Religious Education and was among the first collaborators in the original development of RENEW.

A Church for the New Millennium

MONSIGNOR THOMAS A. KLEISSLER, a priest of the Archdiocese of Newark, was one of the founders of the original RENEW process. Monsignor Kleissler has played a key role in the implementation of RENEW in well over 200 dioceses in the United States and throughout the world. In this capacity he has contributed to articles in many periodicals and newspapers on small Christian community development, scripture sharing, evangelization, lay leadership, justice and shared responsibility. He co-authored with two other RENEW staff members *Small Christian Communities, A Vision of Hope, Resources for Small Christian Communities: A Vision of Hope* and a video by the same name. These are based on his parish experience, his personal involvement in RENEW, and his extensive travel nationally and internationally for RENEW. His world view of church, especially in the area of small Christian community development as a style of parish life, continues to shape parish life today.

The Passionateness of Being: A Meditation

MSGR. RICHARD M. LIDDY is a professor in the Religious Studies Department of Seton Hall University in New Jersey. Previously he taught philosophy and was spiritual director of the Immaculate Conception Seminary in the Archdiocese of Newark. He was also the spiritual director of the North American College in Rome. Presently he is a Fellow of the Woodstock Theological Center in Washington, D.C. where he is working on various projects concerning the work of Bernard Lonergan. Recently he published a work on Lonergan entitled *Transforming Light: Intellectual Conversion in the Early Lonergan* (Liturgical Press, 1993).

Universe Reveals God's Secrets

MARY C. McGUINNESS, O.P., a Caldwell Dominican, coordinates the work of the Small Christian Community Department at the international Office of RENEW, Plainfield, NJ. Her publications include *Small Christian Communities: A Vision of Hope, Resources for Small Christian Communities: A Vision of Hope* and a videotape: *Small Christian Communities: A Vision of Hope*, written collaboratively with Msgr. Thomas A. Kleissler and Margo A. LeBert. She is currently project director for a new series of books to be used by members of small Christian communities. She is actively involved in North American Forum for Small Christian Communities and Buena Vista.

Education: Keystone to Success

SR. MARGUERITE O'CONNOR, S.N.D. has spent most of her life working with the young and the old. She worked with the Blacks at St. Martin de Porres School in New Haven for several years, after which she was asked to work with the elderly in Maine under Archbishop Gerety. She then worked with the elderly in her own Congregation of Notre Dame. She traveled to the provinces in the East, then to California and then to Ohio. She currently works with the AIDS babies in Newark, N.J. She worked under and with Archbishop Gerety in New Haven and Maine. Hers is a life devoted to the needy wherever she was called as a Sister of Notre Dame.

The Option for the Poor

THE REVEREND CASSIAN J. YUHAUS, C.P. H.E.D., former President of CARA (Center for Applied Research in the Apostolate) of Washington, DC, has been engaged with religious communities in the process of renewal since the close of Vatican II. Previous to his position as President, Father Cassian coordinated the Religious Life Program at CARA. While there, his efforts were constantly directed toward expanding the research services CARA renders to the church. He was Co-Founder and Executive Director of the Institute for World Concerns at Duquesne University, an institute sponsored by the Congregation of the Holy Spirit to explore the survival issues of our day. Father Cassian is also the founder and director of the International Institute for Religious now in its twenty-fifty year.

He is editor and coordinator of the best selling book *Religious Life: The Challenge for Tomorrow*. His earlier book *The Catholic Church and American Culture* has been well received. Currently he is writing a book on the Universal Synod of 1994, dedicated to "The Consecrated Life."